FIVE &
EIGHTY
HAMLETS

Shakespeare Memorial Theatre
The English Theatre
Up From the Lizard
We'll Hear a Play
Stratford-upon-Avon
The Theatre Since 1900
The Story of Bath
Drama 1945–50
Down To the Lion
Printer to the House
 (*with E. M. King*)
A Play To-night
The Stratford Festival
 (*with T. C. Kemp*)
Dramatists of Today
Edith Evans
Theatre Programme (*ed*)
Mr Macready
Sybil Thorndike
Verse Drama Since 1800
Paul Scofield
The Night Has Been Unruly
Alec Clunes
The Gay Twenties: A Decade of
 the Theatre
Benson and the Bensonians
The Turbulent Thirties
A Sword for a Prince
John Neville
The Birmingham Repertory
 Theatre

Shakespeare on the English Stage,
 1900–1964
Lamb's Tales (*ed and completed:*
 Nonesuch)
Drama in Britain 1951–64
The Drama Bedside Book
 (*with H. F. Rubinstein*)
Macready's Journals (*ed*)
Robert Donat
The Pomping Folk
Shakespeare Country
Shakespeare's Plays Today
 (*with Arthur Colby Sprague*)
Peter Brook
Sean: Memoirs of Mrs Eileen
 O'Casey (*ed*)
I Call My Name (*verse pamphlet*)
Portrait of Plymouth
Long Ago (*verse pamphlet*)
Theatre Bedside Book
Tutor to the Tsarevich
Eileen (*ed*)
The Edwardian Theatre
Going to Shakespeare
Nicoll, British Drama (*ed*)
The West Country Book
Companion to Shakespeare
Curtain Calls
 (*ed with Lord Miles*)
The Arts Theatre, London
 (*with Wendy Trewin*)

FIVE & EIGHTY HAMLETS

J. C. Trewin

HUTCHINSON
LONDON MELBOURNE AUCKLAND
JOHANNESBURG

This edition first published in 1987 by Hutchinson, an imprint of
Century Hutchinson Ltd, Brookmount House, 62–65 Chandos Place,
London WC2N 4NW

Century Hutchinson Australia Pty Ltd
PO Box 496, 16–22 Church Street, Hawthorn, Victoria 3122, Australia

Century Hutchinson New Zealand Limited
PO Box 40–086, Glenfield, Auckland 10, New Zealand

Century Hutchinson South Africa (Pty) Ltd
PO Box 337, Berglvei, 2012 South Africa

British Library Cataloguing in Publication Data

Trewin, J. C.
  Five and eighty Hamlets.
  1. Shakespeare, William. Hamlet
  2. Shakespeare, William —— Stage history
  —— 1800–1950   3. Shakespeare, William
  —— Stage history —— 1950–
  I. Title
  792.9'5   PR2807

  ISBN 0–09–170900–8

Photoset by Deltatype, Ellesmere Port
Printed and bound in Great Britain by
Anchor Brenden Ltd, Tiptree, Essex

CONTENTS

TO WENDY
WHO SAW MOST OF THEM

The publishers would like to thank the following for allowing photographs to be used in this edition:

The Raymond Mander and Joe Mitchenson Theatre Collection; Angus McBean; the National Film Archive; Gordon Goode for the Shakespeare Birthplace Trust; Donald Cooper.

Whilst every effort has been made to trace copyright, this has not always been possible. The publishers would like to apologise in advance for any invoncenience caused.

INTRODUCTION

*H*AMLET, *Prince of Denmark*, is the world's most famous play. Certainly more has been written about it than any other. It has to be significant that extracts from it occupy eighteen columns in our principal quotation dictionary. It might have been just as reasonable to have reprinted the entire text, though this editor or that, after years with an academic magnifying-glass, would still have argued indefinitely over word and phrase. Progressively detailed studies pack the shelves, from *Some Remarks on the Tragedy of Hamlet* (1736), believed to be Thomas Hanmer's, to the latest Arden edition of the tragedy (1982), edited by Professor Harold Jenkins. There has been debate on every minute in what C. E. Montague, of the *Manchester Guardian*, called long ago 'this monstrous Gothic castle of a poem, with its baffled half-lights and glooms'.

Then why another book? Merely because, as one of the oldest practising drama critics, I must have spent more time listening to *Hamlet* in the theatre than to anything else and there are things I would like, wistfully, to recall. They are not, I insist, academic. They speak for someone who has grown up with the play in performance and who, without obediently looking for relevance, has seen it used to mirror the modern world: thus, the 'angry' generation, so voluble at the end of the 1950s and later, had its own 'angry' Hamlets.

Let me say, very briefly, what the book is not. It is not a history of acting since Burbage. Every major tragedian has played Hamlet, and a host of minor ones, often minnows in

the style of Dickens's Mr Wopsle (*Great Expectations*) who
appeared, catastrophically, under the name of Walden-
garver. It has been in the 'personal pack' of artists as young
as Master Betty (whom unaccountably I missed), transient
Infant Phenomenon of the Regency period, and as old as Sir
Frank Benson whom I did see when he was with the play on
his farewell tours, at seventy-two a courteous phantom.
Often a phrase can speak for artists I never met: Johnston
Forbes-Robertson, with a voice that was likened raptur-
ously to the trumpets of the morning and the flutes of the
evening; H. B. Irving, whose son, Laurence, writing in *The
Precarious Crust*, described him as 'a man of imagination
called upon to be a man of action – certainly neither
madman nor metaphysician'; or Colin Keith-Johnston – his
plus-fours were enough for a popular headline – in a
modern-dress experiment (1925) which shocked people
into argument as over a new play.

A new play is what, in essence, it has become during the
sixty-five years I have been watching and listening – maybe
I should add those first years of reading after I found the
book suddenly during a Cornish winter, at the age of eight.
For centuries the stereotype, though great actors of the
British line transfigured it, was of a 'moody' or 'gloomy'
Dane, soliloquising in slow motion, hand on heart, or
staring glumly at the skull of Yorick. That was not
altogether outmoded when I reached the theatre as a
schoolboy. Today, what the drama critic and sometime
editor of the *Observer*, Ivor Brown, used to dismiss in
conversation as tear-bottle Hamlets, are lost in the night-
wrack: it can be noon in the monstrous Gothic castle.

Every man is said to have something in him of the
endlessly interpretable Hamlet: one reason for the play's
attraction. Another, which can be overlooked in argument,
is its excitement as a dramatic narrative; excitement
restored on goodness knows how many theatre nights. I

have written the book, so generously suggested by Richard
Cohen (whose patience has been sovereign) to remind
myself of these things, of the changing mirror, the
changing climate and lighting: an impression, quite
informal, of the Hamlets in my life, how the play has
sounded, how sometimes it has looked, what has happened
to the man whom the actor-critic, Harley Granville-
Barker, called 'rash and lonely': in short, to chart tone and
temper during my own experience. Since first going to the
theatre, and long before this in the usual domestic run, I
have had a way of remembering voices. It has invariably
been so with Shakespeare, certainly with *Hamlet*. In the
mind I can still play through various scenes as they were
spoken many years ago. There is no question at all of
reproducing the sounds vocally. This is entirely a mental
record: I might say with Antonio, at the outset of *The
Merchant of Venice*, 'How I caught it, found it, or came by it
. . . whereof it is born, I am to learn.' It has been suggested
that, having stammered quite badly, the legacy of an early
illness, I was used to concentrated listening rather than
talking. Moreover, having read Shakespeare years before
hearing him from the stage, I wanted desperately to know
how the plays were spoken, to confirm or correct my ideas.
Speaking once heard would stick, the good and the bad.
Naturally, with experience, I began to sort it out, to
compare the spoken shape of one performance with
another, their emphases, pauses, idiosyncrasies, pace; and
these things have been stored in a listening-bank over the
years.

When I think of *Hamlet*, autobiography keeps breaking
in, not I hope irrelevantly: this begins with a boy in the deep
provinces for whom a hobby became an obsession and ends
with a veteran who knows that comparison can never cease.
How, say, does Hamlet stress 'in your philosophy' to
Horatio after the second Ghost scene? With Rosencrantz

and Guildenstern (II.2)★ does he search for the word, avoiding dangerous glibness, in 'What, to me, is this *quintessence* of dust'? Does he stab at the empty throne on the cry of 'Vengeance!' midway through 'O, what a rogue and peasant slave' (II.2), or later, in the Closet (III.4), seize the locket that the Queen is wearing? Not, perhaps, too much of this: it is a habit the actor William Charles Macready noted gloomily in his journal (January 8, 1835): 'The prescriptive criticism of this country, in looking for particular points instead of contemplating one entire character, abates my confidence in myself.' There is, I agree, a danger in searching for points. A Hamlet may be as thick with them as quills upon the fretful porpentine; but do they add up to the character or to a perambulating prompt copy?

Never mind. This is not, I must repeat, an exercise from the study; it lives in the theatre. Many scholars, abandoning their seclusion, have now recognised the need, as Granville-Barker insisted, for examining the texts in performance as well as in abstract theory. Here I am merely suggesting what one watcher has noticed since the Folio came to life upon a shabbily-mounted stage one spring night in 1922: 'Actus Primus. Scena Prima. Enter Barnardo and Francisco, two centinels.' Then: 'Who's there? – Nay, answer me. Stand and unfold yourself.' That first question-and-answer at curtain-rise (a phrase, I fear, no longer valid) in the night and silence, the cold darkness of the platform before the castle, was overwhelming. It remains so, though in the vagaries of fashion the great prelude is sometimes cut: the play can begin with Claudius recollecting his dear brother's death at what used to be a Court assembly and today, as often as not, is a Privy Council.

★ The text used here is from Professor Peter Alexander's edition of *William Shakespeare: The Complete Works*, published in 1951 and reprinted on many occasions

Through the decades I have learned to watch for cutting: to recognise the familiar pattern of a short text that takes over three hours, and now (far more frequently) to applaud the complete version, startling when Forbes-Robertson did it in London during the late 1890s. Soon afterwards Frank Benson chose at Stratford to stage the 'eternity' in two parts, afternoon and evening, ending the first at the Play scene. Even then the performance was textually flawed: all a nervous young Matheson Lang, as Voltimand, Danish ambassador to Norway, could remember were his first line and his last: 'Most fair return of greetings and desires / As therein are set down.'

Cuts then – and what of the play's aspect and its accelerated pace? We wonder at any revival whether its people will be revenants from an archaic revenge-drama – very seldom now – or Elizabethans of Shakespeare's own world, or brought forward in time, possibly to a Winterhalter-Gothic castle or a Ruritanian court. And the pace? With sets that are both permanent and flexible, there are no longer darkened waits for the changing of nothing in particular. Speech has moved from sonorous declamation to a rapid naturalism. New audiences say that the verse does not suffer. Such a listener as John Mortimer says it does. During an essay in *The Ages of Gielgud* (1984) he regrets the throwing-away of 'To be, or not to be' in 'a furtive and tuneless monotone, as though the greatest danger . . . were to allow the audience to recognise a familiar quotation.'

With actor-managers gone, directors have the last word. It is for them to rule method and manner. As far back as 1937, at the Westminster Theatre, Michael MacOwan experimented with Professor Dover Wilson's textual ideas (general verdict: interesting but unproven). In the same year Tyrone Guthrie – his Hamlet, Laurence Olivier, agreeing with him – had staged the play in terms of Freudian theory, the Oedipus complex, at the Old Vic and

Elsinore. Little more at the time was heard of that, but experiment is unstemmed, the text constantly combed for surprises: a student-Hamlet (1965), blond and scarfed, or the Graveyard scene transferred to a charnel-house, or a Hamlet soliloquising in the Players' property-skip and allowing the lid to fall on him.

Most of the characters have been reconsidered in our day: the King and Queen, who used to be stiff playing-cards; the Ghost, sometimes conceivably from another world and not a suffering elocutionist in this; Polonius, recognisably a reliable elder statesman; Ophelia (so many have defied criticism) seldom a faint water-colour. People practically forgotten have asserted themselves: Reynaldo ('My lord, I have') since Alec Guinness discovered him in 1937; Fortinbras, who should end the play nobly; the Second Gravedigger, who may fetch stoups from Yaughan, but whom we have known also as a supercilious sacristan. In the complete text (V.2), but not in the filleted version, we discover the fate of Guildenstern and Rosencrantz ('Why, man, they did make love to this employment; they are not near my conscience').

But Hamlet himself must be supreme, that protean Prince who is the 'observ'd of all observers'. I have met some five and eighty: though the phrase, with its borrowed rhythm, may alarm an accountant, it is a fair statement of personal premières (taking in one film, a ballet, and the curiosity, *Fratricide Punished*.) A few performances have slipped into the dark, no shred remaining: mercifully one travesty where the first interval could not come too soon. These do not matter. Such Hamlets, all differing, as John Gielgud, Ernest Milton, Laurence Olivier and Paul Scofield remain in my heart of hearts from the world's most celebrated play, its most contentious, above all its most exciting. Excitement has been the key: in a lost provincial theatre, on the Stratford stages, in a Danish ballroom at

Marienlyst on a stormy summer night. It was the key in last week's production, and should be in tomorrow's. Very simply: 'This is I, Hamlet the Dane.' At every hearing we ask ourselves if the actor who says this can justify the claim, and why.

Hampstead, 1987

I
FIRST NIGHT: 1908–22

I

IT BEGAN, I suppose, in the farthest south of Cornwall, at the end of the Lizard peninsula's all-but-island,
not to be confused with Penwith in the haze across
Mount's Bay. On a very wet December evening towards
Christmas in 1916, rain was driving straight from the sea –
or, as my father would insist, approximately from Brazil –
above the crags of Old Lizard Head; thence, over a small
barley-field and our sunken kitchen-garden, to beat a
rataplan on the windows of Kynance Bay House.

I had been lying on a bearskin rug before the dining-
room fire: an eight-year-old's last hour before bed, with
what we knew as 'coarse weather' shut out behind thick
scarlet curtains. I reached up on tip-toe to the three
bookshelves above the fireplace, possibly to take down
Lew Wallace's *Ben-Hur* (ribbed green cloth) for the sake of
its chariot race; 'When the Byzantine and the Christian were
halfway down the course, Ben-Hur turned the first goal
and the race was *won*' (in exuberant italics). If not this, it
might have been Harrison Ainsworth's *Old St Paul*'s
(brown and gilt), with its cascade of molten lead that
flooded the vaults beneath the blazing cathedral: 'The two
partners in iniquity, and the whole of their ill-gotten gains,
were buried in the boiling waves.'

Whichever it was, and I fancy now it must have been

Ainsworth, the shelves were so tightly packed that I had to tug very hard. The book that did fall suddenly was something I had not met before with any interest, a complete *Shakespeare*. After his last leave my merchant-captain father, iced up that winter in the port of Archangel during the middle of the First World War, had left the book behind with a pack of others. It was his habit, on any new voyage, to exchange one collection for another, as much as would fill a couple of fair-sized crates. His taste was catholic, so the claw-legged mahogany bookcase in our hall had been given over to such works as *The Stones of Venice* (volumes one and three; the second had vanished); a big *History of Newfoundland* in acid-green boards, probably sold to Father at St John's by its resolute local author, Judge Prowse, a publicist for his own work; a fourth volume, *Leila* included, of the novels of Bulwer Lytton, 'Excellent tale' scribbled on its last fly-leaf; *Mrs Caudle's Curtain Lectures*, disappointing, I thought; an arid *Life of Gladstone*, a medley of Hesba Stretton, Joseph Conrad and Mrs Henry Wood; and a set of Dickens that lacked *Nicholas Nickleby* and *Edwin Drood*: I would get to them later.

By now I had tried most of these with mixed success. It was hard to imagine Father reading the *Shakespeare* on any ocean or in any port. A curious production, it was bound in black leather and had a smugly irritating format, pages in double-column framed in pink, with a vertical pink line between the columns. That night it flopped open on the rug at one of the last plays I would meet in the theatre, the First Part of *Henry VI* and the Westminster Abbey funeral of Henry V:

> Hung be the heavens with black, yield day to-night!
> Comets, importing change of times and states,
> Brandish your crystal tresses in the sky . . .

Presently, in my westward-looking attic, surrounded by

eccentrically maritime wallpaper, and exploring by the glimmer of a night-light under an egg-shaped glass, I found myself, round page 1200 or so, at *Pericles, Prince of Tyre* which seemed to be kept deliberately aside. This, I discovered after some years, was because the editor, taking it to be only part-Shakespearian, had refused snobbishly to let it join its betters: snobbishly indeed, I thought twenty-three years on, after seeing Robert Eddison, with his lyric voice and bearing, as Pericles upon the lawn of the Open Air Theatre in Regent's Park.

That was far off. At the age of eight I was unused to reading plays. No one in the family was interested in the theatre except my elder sister Iris, then a VAD nurse at Exeter, an address so distant that it might have been Greenland. My father would have been no help whatever: persuaded against all reason and argument that he had heard Melba singing in *Iolanthe*, he wisely stopped there, not that I would have known one way or the other. Battling on for a few nights in the attic, and scarcely encouraged by an aunt who glanced at the book, said curtly, 'Made to be told,' and handed it back, I could do little with *Pericles* until I reached the passage where the goddess Diana appears to the sleeping King. I thought then that his cry, 'Celestial Dian, goddess argentine!' (a word to be looked up) was wildly exciting. Ready to share it, I ran through the village, addressing the least likely people, who said 'The boy's mazed!' and walked on.

Mazed or not, I continued to read, never fortified, and I was sorry about this, by my Landewednack schoolmaster (Landewednack was the name of our 'Church town'). His own taste inclined to *Silas Marner* and he thought me tiresomely precocious. Still, I went on fighting with blank verse that sounded blanker when read aloud to the coast-guards' notched look-out pole on Old Lizard Head, which in those days received my confidences and had been greeted as celestial Dian. Presently it would hear, among quantities of the text, that *Hamlet, Prince of Denmark* was the best of the plays as well as the simplest. It puzzled me why there should be any trouble about it. Hamlet's uncle, Claudius, had murdered his King and brother, the elder Hamlet, pouring poison in his ear while the man slept in the orchard. Thereupon Claudius would seize the throne of Denmark and marry the widowed Queen Gertrude, young Hamlet's mother. Obviously – for I believed firmly in the super-natural and had a Lizard experience of my own – the murdered King's ghost had returned one winter night to tell the story to his son upon the ramparts of the royal castle. (I thought of it, roughly, as St Michael's Mount.) The Prince would have his revenge on Claudius, even if, to keep the play going, he took some time about it. In the end several people were dead: an eavesdropping politician, Polonius; his daughter Ophelia, whom Hamlet had cast off and who drowned herself in madness; her brother Laertes, who fought a last duel with Hamlet; Queen Gertrude; and Hamlet himself ('The rest is silence'). Not really difficult for a young reader totally unconcerned with ethical and textual problems but ready for a good plot and the sound of the verse. A speech by Hamlet's friend, who had been with him at the university ('What make you from Wittenberg, Horatio?'), appealed to me at once:

> What if it tempt you toward the flood, my lord,
> Or to the dreadful summit of the cliff
> That beetles o'er his base into the sea? . . .
> The very place puts toys of desperation,
> Without more motive, into every brain
> That looks so many fathoms to the sea
> And hears it roar beneath.

That could have been written for me. To my father's disbelief – he had been bred in sail – I had no head for heights

and would do anything rather than step on a fairly low first
floor window-sill. But from early childhood I had been
accustomed to the sombre range of the Lizard cliffs and its
plummet drops: Penolver Point, where a Norwegian
barque, *Hansy*, was wrecked, spinning and lurching in a
November gale, or the loom of Rill Head above Kynance.
It was from there that the galleons of Medina Sidonia (a girl
in the village had Sidonia as her first name) were sighted on
a summer afternoon in 1588. Clearly, granted that he
would have had to provide his own castle, ours was a world
where Hamlet could conceivably have lived.

I tried several other plays, even *Love's Labour's Lost*: what
on earth did the jokes mean? 'If sore be sore, than L to sore
makes fifty sores of sorel.' It was *Hamlet* that grew into an
obsession. Iris, at home now, read it to me during an
autumn convalescence when for nearly six months I could
not go to school far up in Plymouth. I was wholly
ungrateful for a gift of *Lamb's Tales*. Charles's paraphrasing, if it was his, was simply tepid: 'The top of one
dreadful cliff.' About then it troubled me, in a drive at
Dickens, to read of Wopsle's Hamlet in *Great Expectations*:
'My gifted townsman stood gloomily apart with folded
arms, and I could have wished that his curls and forehead
had been more probable.' I refused to credit this as a likely
picture of any Hamlet in the theatre. Not, of course, that I
should ever see the play acted: Lizard Town, a portentous
name for our lazy straggle where, on the Green, serpen-
tine-workers' wheels churred all day, had nothing to do
with the pomping folk (a phrase native to southern
Cornwall). Agreed, as any stage-struck crow might fly, it
was only round twenty miles from the place, behind St
Ives, where the boy John Henry Brodribb, who became
Henry Irving, had been brought up. Very much nearer, a
couple of miles from us along the 'double hedge' top, the
village of Ruan Minor had a Rectory lawn on which, ages

before, Johnston Forbes Robertson and Helena Modjeska had played the balcony scene of *Romeo and Juliet* under a harvest moon. In maybe 1918 the primeval recollection would not have stirred me: I had no idea that Forbes-Robertson (with the hyphen slipped in) had grown into the Hamlet of his time; that, unusually, he had died upon the Danish throne, grasping the crown, and that he had restored to the acted text Fortinbras, Prince of Norway, one of the high assembly of Shakespeare's Princes.

Nobody would have bothered at the Lizard for half a minute. I understood that the theatre belonged to another world, and we should be happy to stay in our remoteness away from the teeming metropolitan life, the reckless abandon, of Camborne. Yet, having performed Nelson, with telescope and prickly epaulettes, in *Mrs Jarley's Waxworks* at the Reading Room, I felt secretly that I knew a bit about the theatre. The cinema, too, had touched us. Had not *Uncle Tom's Cabin* arrived in its tin boxes on an evening when first customers waited patiently on the Beacon for the Reading Room to open (trouble with the 'limelight') and Little Eva expired upside down on her wrinkled screen? All right, as far as it went; but I could not imagine anything going as far as *Hamlet*.

II

At heart I had not wished to live anywhere else, and at that age never dreamt I would. My father, who had been over fifty at my birth, decided otherwise. The last man for the small change of retirement, he resolved (we thought unwisely) to leave the sea, so I had no chance, as my mother and sisters had, to travel with him to some strange fold of the map, the Crimea perhaps, Iquique, Callao, Rosario. Obsessively, I would have liked Denmark; a final voyage, not with me, was to Sweden. It was, ironically, for my benefit that Father chose to settle near, and then in, Plymouth where I had had tentative school terms. Plymouth was a lovable and grandly historic port, yet at first I missed the Lizard sadly, every jut and pinnacle of rock, the spreading arc of Pentreath surf, burnished copper in a farm kitchen, the serpentine's olive and brooding red. Much else: our brambled lane to the sea, cliff carpets of mesembryanthemum (properly 'Sally-me-'ansome'), the Landewednack rookery, one haunted, mounded meadow. It hurt, but soon there would be compensations: a schoolmaster who could quote from *Hamlet* and often did; and especially, next door to us, Colonel H. G. Le Mesurier, who was afterwards a fastidious Oxford lexicographer. He knew a good deal about the Shakespearian stage and the text of *Hamlet* as heard in the theatre then – or as he heard it; I had still to get there.

The tragedy, I gathered, could have been performed originally in 1600/1601. Of two printed Quarto versions, a first, 'pirated' in 1603, seems to have rested largely on the memory of a player. Almost certainly, the man had acted Marcellus (and one or two smaller parts, perhaps) and had got scenes right in which he appeared himself; otherwise, optimistic paraphrasing. The Second Quarto (1604) was probably from the original manuscript, and often in performance we had a mingling of this with the First Folio version of 1623, a revised playhouse text. Theorists had never ceased to debate comma by comma. 'Don't let that worry you too much,' said Le Mesurier cheerfully, as he went on to talk about various things to watch or listen for in the theatre. Difficult no doubt, in the first scene (presuming the lines are uncut) to know just what Horatio means when he exclaims of the Ghost, 'So frown'd he once when, in an angry parle, / He smote the sledded pollax on the ice.' Polacks or poleaxe? But Hamlet's 'Then saw you not his face?' to Horatio and Marcellus in the third scene: is this a statement or a question? In the Queen's Closet (III.4), at 'Look here upon this picture and on this,' does Hamlet seize the Queen's locket and compare its picture of Claudius with his own locket-miniature of his father (presumably the original stage business), or indicate portraits on the tapestry, or leave everything to the mind's eye? Other questions as well: Le Mesurier was a ready observer. It pleased him too, if sparing me any prolonged exegesis, to discuss Hamlet's character, a man living in perpetual mental fight while Elsinore darkened round him.

I heard of the procession of players since, presumably, Richard Burbage at Shakespeare's Globe Theatre on Bankside: Thomas Betterton, of the Restoration stage, who when he saw the Ghost, turned as white as his neckcloth; David Garrick, also at his most mesmeric on the ramparts; the stately John Philip Kemble; Edmund Kean, against whom – I am told, inexplicably – I developed a lasting prejudice; William Charles Macready, Charles Fechter, and Sir Henry Irving; Sir Herbert Tree, who had a celestial choir, sometimes out of tune, to sing him to his rest; and Sir Johnston Forbes-Robertson (Romeo of Ruan Minor), who had retired prematurely in 1913. Comparatively recent, he could dominate memory: 'But you should have *heard* Forbes-Robertson.' I did once in a late recording that, if slightly avuncular – and with a single unexpected lapse on a vowel sound – attained a fine nobility, a reproof to the walking neuroses presently to be fashionable. I saw him also in an early and embarrassing silent film, Hamlet hurrying across a Dorset beach.

Le Mesurier had not seen this, I believe. In his *Hamlet* lore he would tell me of such an oddity as Barry Sullivan's Victorian reading of 'I know a hawk from a handsaw' (heronshaw) which he spoke as 'I know a hawk from a herne. Pshaw!' Then there was ancient and ridiculous business long discarded: that for the First Gravedigger, who removed a number of assorted waistcoats before beginning to dig while, as fast as he took them off, his Second Gravedigger snatched them and put them on.

Somebody lent me collected reviews of Henry Irving at the Lyceum, written by Clement Scott and entitled, firmly, *From 'The Bells' to 'King Arthur'*. There I read that typically unhurried notice of *Hamlet* in 1874: 'The scene changes to a dazzling interior, broken in its artistic lines and rich with architectural beauty: the harps sound, the procession is commenced. The jewels, and crowns, and sceptres dazzle, and at the end of the train comes Hamlet . . . a man and a Prince in thick robed silk and a jacket, or paletot, edged with fur: a tall, imposing figure, so well-dressed that nothing distracts the eye from the wonderful face.' The last two words suggested that this was a genuine Hamlet, no Wopsle-Waldengarver parody. I had never heard of Clement Scott who, as a spare-time seaside versifier, would one day be Max Beerbohm's victim ('It is fearful to think of his soul being slowly crushed by so uncongenial a life'). But as *Daily Telegraph* drama critic of the Lyceum era, when he would settle to his two thousand meandering words after supper, he was obviously a pontiff to envy.

Well-dressed or not, I liked the idea of the Lyceum *Hamlet*. Alas, it belonged to history. I had still to catch the tragedy acted, and time ticked away: after all, I was past eleven. At that period Cornwall, just across the Tamar, had only (and by no means invariably) its itinerant players or, as I would write later, 'pomping folk from the market square, / The night, the booth, the torches' flare.' Yet, though Plymouth possessed a splendid Theatre Royal at the very end of the touring system, where was the professional Shakespeare for it? Loftily, I barely condescended to *A Little Bit of Fluff*. Having at that age to develop a passion for something, whatever it was, I took on Gilbert and Sullivan, mainly because my younger sister had married the musical

director of the second D'Oyly Carte company – an
occupation that Father dismissed as regrettable – and I could
count on annual visits. I did my best with Gilbert, even,
against Le Mesurier's advice, reading the straight plays. His
contempt for Shakespeare, especially *Hamlet*, puzzled me.
It was visible in the libretto of a non-Savoy opera, *The
Mountebanks*, the dumbshow, and a song that, as Sir Arthur
Quiller-Couch ('Q'), who was revered in the West
Country, would say, sought to drag the very weeds and
mud out of Ophelia's end:

> When she heard he wouldn't wed her,
> In a river, in a medder,
> Took a header, and a deader
>   Was Oph-e-li-a!

'Q' regarded this as lamentable. Luckily, maybe, there
was no chance to see *The Mountebanks* in operation. A first
visit to London had done nothing for the classics. I had to be
less lofty than in Plymouth, being taken to the eternal *Chu-
Chin-Chow* which left little behind it except a large camel
against an unlikely moon; and to *Kissing Time* when Leslie
Henson, with a face that needed ironing, was hurled upon
the Winter Garden stage from an exploding motor-car
(off). No Shakespeare: in fact, for me not a trace of *Hamlet*
until, during a gusty spring week as late as 1922, a
provincial impresario named Harold V. Neilson (born
Thomas Clegg) brought to Plymouth one of his various
'festivals'. Fourth night, or possibly fifth: *Hamlet, Prince of
Denmark*.

2
WHO'S THERE?: 1922

I

THESE festivals were festive only in the sense that,
with eight plays during a week – six nights, two
matinees – it would be possible, given the desire and
the capital, to luxuriate: pit, early doors, one shilling and
tenpence. Twenty minutes before the start, one shilling and
threepence, but this small saving meant that you might be
in a limbo at the back of the pit, beneath the overhang of the
dress-circle, and with sight and hearing gravely impaired.
In a Shakespeare week (I would discover) this was not often
a problem because Plymouth people, as a whole – if not the
local Shakspere Society which clung to its spelling – had
then no noticeable wish to luxuriate. The town (elevated to
a city in the late 1920s) was predominantly musical, with a
distinguished Symphony Orchestra and an unwavering
love of 'celebrity concerts'. The stage had to be secondary,
even though any dilettante had plenty of choice: the gallant
Repertory, its stage like a tea-tray poised on an unseen
spiral stair; a respected music hall, the Palace, in the middle
of Union Street, the sailors' traditional parade; and three
lesser houses, given to the shoddier skirts-and-flirts revue,
Ruritanian or domestic melodrama, and more curiously
assembled Variety bills.

Plymouth should certainly have been prouder than it was
of the Royal, 'rising in column'd pride and Attic grace',

though relatively few people would speak of it in those terms. It formed part of an apparently perpetual steel engraving, the architect John Foulston's glimmering, white-plastered Ionic-pillared block of hotel (to the east) and theatre (to the north). Built during the Regency on what had been the blossoming slope of a cherry garden, and holding over 1,200, it had had more than a century of reasonably profitable life. Now, controlled – 'Sole Managing Director' – by an eminence rarely on view, J. M. (Jimmy) Glover, once a formidable musical director of Drury Lane and Mayor of Bexhill-on-Sea, it was, in jargon I picked up from my brother-in-law, a 'Number Two' date for secondary touring companies (*Paddy, the Next Best Thing, Sally, Love Among the Paint Pots, Up in Mabel's Room*, and so forth). Doubtless; but it seemed perfect to me: within, a courtly green-and-gold auditorium of four tiers; stalls, and behind them the pit, separated by a wooden barrier topped by red American cloth; dress- and upper circles, and a high gallery, an eyrie for any eagle that happened to drop in while passing. One stared at a drop-curtain of the Battle of Trafalgar, a crowded composition signed in the right-hand bottom corner by an artist named H. Pedgeon. Behind it, and beyond an ample stage, the Royal had so much unused space, with mixed shipyard smells of size and glue and old rope, that it might have been possible to lay down a three-decker.

I hunted for the Royal's history and was delighted when Le Mesurier remembered a story, told by Squire Bancroft, of a veteran player from mid-Victorian stock. Should his lines elude him, a frequent dilemma, he would exclaim to anybody on stage with him: 'Go to! Thou weariest me! Take this purse of gold, provide thyself with richer habiliments, and meet me at my lodging straight.' Whereupon he would leave with dignity and let his partner get on with it: awkward, one might think, if it were a current comedy, but no trouble for a Victorian professional for whom the readiness was all. I asked myself whether this would ever have been noticed in the middle of a *Hamlet* and decided that some in the audience might have accepted it quite cheerfully.

II

Neilson's festival company, so I would learn one day, had been rapidly stitched together and directed, with his own textual cuts, by Ben Greet. Much loved, he had been at the birth of 'Old Vic' Shakespeare: this was just before the First World War when Lilian Baylis, dictator of the popular house (officially the Royal Victoria Hall) at the corner of Waterloo Road and the New Cut, decided that Shakespeare might very well be part of her programme as well as 'Opera in English'. Greet knew everything about touring the plays which he would present as serenely in a public park as in a major theatre. At the Royal, in the ebb of a cold February, I encountered a first Shakespeare, *The Tempest*, which now lives simply for its shipwreck: the gleam through the darkness of a single red lantern swung from a crazily tossing pole against a grey curtain. (Within three decades the best young director of his time would be praised for his imagination in devising much the same effect at Stratford.) Plainly I must have enjoyed the night because it angered me when a cynical child – though older than I was – left the theatre with a frigid 'Wasting our time, I call it – wasting our time!' and jumped upon a Compton tramcar with an uninhibited flourish of the left foot. It was almost as withering as a judgment by a former neighbour of ours at the Lizard. On a rare visit to Plymouth this young man sat bleakly through Maugham's *Our Betters*, the most daring comedy the author had written, and dismissed it in a monosyllable, 'Dry!'

I am not sure if he would have said this of *Hamlet*. To hear it rising from the text and, in an American critic's phrase, to see an actor who had 'drawn on the black tights of the classic Scandinavian', was so deep an excitement that minor trials – a bronchial audience, draughts chilling the pit, tramcars clanging outside – scarcely ruffled me. In Greet's production the 'platform' before the castle was a range of bulkily-bunched curtains, odd in that Castle Dangerous, but I questioned nothing when Bernardo (more often during the years, Barnardo) spoke the two words, 'Who's there?' which ushered in three hours of airs from heaven and blasts from hell.

The same curtains, unbunched and against a frayed tapestry, represented the royal Court of Denmark. A moment's pang there, for, in spite of Le Mesurier's warning, I had expected the richer habiliments of Irving, that dazzling interior and 'architectural beauty'. No jewels or sceptres, simply a throne, a chair or two, and a huddle of patently empty cardboard goblets untouched until the close of the night. Hamlet did not arrive at the tail of a procession but was already seated, tactfully not centre-stage but very near it; he wore what I came to recognise as the customary black tunic and tights, lavishly romantic open-collared shirt, and gold neck chain. Well-dressed? I hoped so. The night was defiantly unpictorial; Ophelia's grave, a tub of earth; more than a hint of economy among the courtiers. Still, I had neither time nor wish to criticise, and remembered only a single matter that Le Mesurier had told me to look for, the comparison of lockets. I did ask vaguely why the King, at all hours, wore an ornate crown too big for him, and Horatio a spruce crimson toga, or so it appeared. I told myself wisely that it was to point one of his final lines, 'More an antique Roman than a Dane'. It might, of course, have been a scholar's gown of the German University of Wittenberg, yet to this day – maybe the dangerous conjecture of an ill-breeding mind – I recall it as a toga.

Quite unimportant: it was Hamlet's play. The actor was Frank Darch, a man of about forty – I never saw him again – with singularly beautiful hands and a gentle, courteous manner. Not, I dare say, more than a direct, untrammelled statement, but enough to preserve the flow of the narrative. I would learn soon that from any Hamlet one phrase lingers, and from Darch I have the passage when, drawing aside the monstrously hirsute First Player, he said with endearing, expectant confidence, 'You could for a need study a speech of some dozen or sixteen lines which I would set down and insert in't, could you not?' (Shakespeare here, talking to a colleague at a Globe rehearsal.) The First Player would, and presumably did.

III

During the ensuing Royal Command Performance (no dumbshow for the King carefully to avoid seeing) we had a few relevant fragments of 'The Mouse-trap'. The *Hamlet* text, I knew even then, had been cut substantially and the programme contained a note candid for the period: 'Owing to the length of the play certain scenes have been omitted.' The result, I learned, was what Le Mesurier had explained as the customary acting script, though there would be one uncommon exception.

What the profession knows as the 'eternity' *Hamlet* occupies four-and-a-half to five hours. Greet's text took about three: it could have been less if the pace had not been so deliberate, the speech sonorous and echoing in the manner of the period (though Darch, who had been with a fastidious director, Bridges-Adams, at Stratford, seldom lapsed). Cuts came from a prompt book based on a coral reef of tradition. Thus we lost much of the talk between

Marcellus and Horatio in the first scene ('Good now, sit down, and tell me, he that knows . . .'); Hamlet's nervous time-filling 'Heavy-headed revel east and west' in scene 4 (perhaps those unpersuasive goblets at court were to suggest heavy-headed revel); the core of the Ghost's narrative ('Whose effect . . . all my smooth body'); the entire Polonius-and-Reynaldo passage too easily regarded as sacrificial; the Ambassadors, Voltimand and Cornelius; the topical 'eyrie of children' in Hamlet's meeting with Rosencrantz and Guildenstern; a lot of the First Player in II.2; the dumbshow; much of 'The Mouse-trap'; the beginning of III.3; the last part of the Closet scene from Hamlet's return on 'One word more' to 'the neighbour room'; much of IV.7, the colloquy between the King and Laertes; the second scene of the fifth act, until 'But I am very sorry, good Horatio, / That to Laertes I forgot myself'; and throughout the night a number of minor cuts. It was remarkable, after all this, that Greet at Plymouth insisted upon the final entrance of Fortinbras of Norway, who arrives as a sun-in-splendour, life in the midst of death, above the stricken court. He was played at the Royal in an immense Viking helmet by an actor named Whitwell Firth, who doubled him with the Ghost. Several in the audience that night must have been surprised by his arrival, especially as they would have missed various early references to him. But then it was assumed that a well-trained audience would know the play and would not grumble: a different attitude from one a quarter of a century later when a Stratford director of *Romeo and Juliet* was sharply reproved for leaving out the Friar's explanation to Juliet about the phial of poison.

Fortinbras is familiar now. I was too young to know in 1922 that Bridges-Adams said, 'His last appearance should stir one like the end of *Götterdämmerung*.' James Agate, for many years from the mid-1920s drama critic of the *Sunday*

Times, held that the man should be at least six feet in height, with gold armour and a voice that would ring through the requiem:

> He was likely, had he been put on,
> To have proved most royal; and for his passage,
> The soldiers' music and the rite of war
> Speak loudly for him.

It would be seven years before I met Fortinbras again. There was a time when small-part men in the Castle of Elsinore would never know what might chance to them in production, even Rosencrantz and Guildenstern; I cannot separate the Ben Greet actors. There is an agreeable, and I hope not apocryphal, story of a production in which an independent north-country Guildenstern, with a grudge against Hamlet, refused to reply, 'I know no touch of them' when asked to play upon the pipes. Saying, in effect, 'Why not?', he danced a brisk hornpipe to his own tune.

There should be a Sailor in *Hamlet*. Indeed, there are 'two seafaring men,' of whom only one addresses Horatio. A Servant, or Gentleman, should bring in the Sailor, or Sailors. Presently, a Messenger delivers letters from Hamlet to the King: 'They were given me by Claudio, he receiv'd them / Of him that brought them.' (It is like Shakespeare's pleasant carelessness with names to have both a Claudius and Claudio at Elsinore.) How much the same functionary can do must depend upon a director's resources in man-power. Later I would know Elsinore to be exceedingly well staffed, but during my Plymouth vigils the Lords, Attendants, Gentlemen, Messengers and Servants were rolled democratically into what Arthur Machen, the Welsh writer who was once in Frank Benson's Shakespearian company, described, in another context, as 'a sort of conglomerate or pudding-stone part'. Dickens had the same notion when he reported Wopsle's Hamlet:

'The noble boy in the ancestral boots was inconsistent, representing himself, as it were in one breath, as an able seaman, a strolling actor, a gravedigger, a clergyman, and a person of the utmost importance at a court fencing match.'

3
HAMLET, THE DANE:
1922–32

I

AFTER the play at the Royal, where the doubling and trebling would have gratified both Machen and Dickens, I sat up all night remembering it. At this remove most of the voices are blurred, though not Darch's gentle tenor which left no line unclarified. It was, as I came to see, a simplification, but it was a plausible one, and when the actor stepped forward in the Graveyard with 'This is I, Hamlet the Dane,' one would not have contradicted him. I cannot summon him now in 'How all occasions', a rarity in the period's short versions: probably Greet believed it would not be missed. From the rest of the evening I can hear the precise response of an Ophelia who looked like a tall lily, and who was called, unluckily, Esme Biddle; the bluster of a Claudius who spoke far louder than anyone – a King, maybe, had a right to do so – and Greet's own cosy dithering with Polonius, a part he must have acted innumerable times without asking (as, in the clench of tradition, I did not for some years) how an old fumbler had reached so high an office of state.

This was Greet's last appearance in Plymouth. It was a period, 1922–4, when several Shakespeare companies were on the crowded road: Charles Doran's, Henry Baynton's, Frank Benson's (back from a South African tour with a new

leading lady, Genevieve Townsend), and others conducted
by Edward Dunstan, who remained in the north, and
Alexander Marsh. The Doran company, in Plymouth
during the early summer of 1922 – an extraordinary year for
Shakespeare at the Royal – was a composite tribute to its
leader's eye for youth. A southern Irishman, only slightly
accented, he was a sound artificer who, as his own
manager, played most of the leading parts himself. His
company, with the future in its eyes, had we but known,
included such players as Edith Sharpe, the young Ralph
Richardson and Donald Woolfitt (the original spelling);
Abraham Sofaer, a natural tragedian who was, surprisingly, Feste; Arthur Young, Norman Shelley, and Neil
Porter. Astonishing; but no Hamlet.

In the next Shakespeare week, that autumn, Hamlet
would be at its heart. He was Henry Baynton, a Warwickshire man of thirty, who had understudied H. B. Irving,
Henry's son, in *The Bells*: a fact that caused James Agate,
not the best of the drama critics, if the most quoted, to write
him off as 'the shadow of a shade'.

The productions, with their heavy black drapes and an
occasional full set, were visually richer than the Neilson/
Greet repertory. Baynton himself ruled. Tall and handsome, physical advantages that Frank Darch had lacked,
and making every possible use of his profile, he leased the
centre of the stage too freely and obtrusively: a born actor
with the evils that could attend it. His voice, a powerful
baritone that was getting rubbed, suffered from vibrato: he
had the period stigmata, extreme slowness, excessive
make-up and the invariable pronunciation of 'my' as 'muh'.
An epigraph for his Hamlet could have been the King's
'Words without thoughts never to heaven go.' Yet, just as
'readable' in a book review can mean anything or nothing,
so one could suggest that Baynton's performance was
'watchable'. He was less appealing than Darch, but nobody

could have charged him with irresolution: a natural melodramatic quality held his audience in the Play and Closet
scenes. Among his cast, and uncommon at that date, Alice
de Grey's Ophelia did not slip on her madness like an
enveloping cloak from the peg; and Percy Vernon had what
any Polonius then could signally lack, a certain stateliness.
Baynton would appear in some London seasons during the
mid-1920s – in his treatment of *The Tempest* young John
Gielgud was Ferdinand – but he slid gradually into the mist.
I saw him again only once when Robert Atkins cast him
(1933) as Capulet in a summer night *Romeo and Juliet* at the
Open Air Theatre, Regent's Park. During the decade since
Plymouth his technique seemed to have weakened; he
hardly belonged to the company as he prowled round the
fringes of the lawn, muttering under his breath, 'Muh
daughter Juliet'.

II

After Baynton we had a year's gap until, in March 1924, I
had my first overwhelming theatrical experience. 'Great',
often implying no more than a night's enthusiasm, is a
word, like 'marvellous' and 'wonderful', to use sparely; but
after sixty years I would still use it for the Hamlet of Ernest
Milton at another of Neilson's 'festivals'. I knew enough to
realise what an exotic figure Milton must have been on the
London stage of the early 1920s, an American actor of
Jewish descent who had settled in England, and who had
conquered the Old Vic with his romantic passion and the
surge of his verse-speaking. There had been much praise,
too, for his bitingly scornful performance in Galsworthy's
Loyalties (not yet seen in Plymouth) as a Jewish outsider, de
Levis, in an anti-Semitic section of London society.

I was not prepared for a man who, within a day or so, had
local Shakespearians, in unexpected numbers, arguing

against him strenuously; a classical actor, they said, who would not stick to the rules of the game. Then thirty-three, dark, searchingly intense, of middle height, in movement lithe, swift and rarely predictable, he was not conventionally handsome. If he never stared across the footlights, Baynton-fashion, his gaze could appear to concentrate on every person in the house, like the eyes of Kitchener in the war-time recruiting poster. Milton could enjoy such a farcical gift as Master Ford in *The Merry Wives of Windsor* with which he began his week, especially when tantalising a commonplace Falstaff with the advances and withdrawals of the bag of gold; but above all else he was a romantic tragedian, a Hamlet that, after his death, Sir Alec Guinness would describe as 'the Renaissance Prince *par excellence*, a man familiar with the ways of mankind . . . who could always see the two sides of a coin, tortured by conscience and burdened by duty, a man of sharp wit but exquisite manners'. His natural nobility was unaffected by grease-paint haughtiness. Idiosyncrasies were clear: the cadenzas on unimportant phrases, a sibilance that more than once could be oddly sinister, vowels that could trail off suddenly like a drooping pennant. But Hamlet was there, so indubitably that from the moment of 'A little more than kin and less than kind' in tones like a sable silver'd, we could have been made free of the play for the first time. On seeing the Ghost he had indeed a supernatural visitation; he became a man possessed. 'Angels and ministers of grace defend us!' was breathed, barely audible, as he swung round from Horatio. When he was left alone on the battlements the haunting cry, 'Hillo! ho! ho! boy! Come, bird, come!' rose as I would never know it again. From the distant night I think still of throat-tightening excitement, of an emotional force sometimes almost demonic. Speech after speech he double-charged. I cannot say at this distance how many *Hamlet* problems he answered, though the voice speaks unblurred. For me, with his felicities and faults, his leaping across every chasm, he governed the stage as the man himself, of 'the courtier's, soldier's, scholar's, eye, tongue, sword'. (An American writer has said here, with comic solemnity, that 'the sense of derangement is heightened by the fact that the order of the genitive nouns does not correspond semantically with the order of the things possessed': not, I imagine, that we lose sleep over it.)

I was not to be put off Milton by derisive local gossip or my housemaster's cynicism. In school one morning I ventured to say how moved I had been: told not to be dogmatic and that Milton was a poor choice for a schoolboy to admire, we returned sternly to Xenophon. Yet, a few months ahead, I knew again what I had seen when Iris gave me Milton's own verse drama, *Christopher Marlowe*, for which Walter de la Mare had written a prologue calling the author 'player himself of Shakespeare, root to crown', and adding: 'The wind has blown too long from out the east, over bleak naturalism's arid wastes.' Though Milton's play was only an actor's relishing exercise, aria upon aria, lines in it reminded me of that Hamlet at the Royal, 'A cry of genius and a flash of art, / And the forgotten cold flame of despair.'

About four decades later, a widower (his wife was the novelist, Naomi Royde-Smith) and retired from the theatre, Milton would visit us in Hampstead from the small hotel where he was living. At well past seventy his voice still swooped and sprang, but one or two fixed beliefs obsessed him: it was impossible to get him to pardon the apparent, and complex, wrongs that A or B or C had done to him during his life on the stage. It was when he turned to Shakespeare that he would change and sound infinitely possessive. 'Hamlet,' he said, lingering on the name; 'I knew the man – you will remember that.' They were almost the last words I heard him speak. He did know the man, and I remembered it.

III

After I had first seen Milton and spent a dazed twenty minutes wandering round Plymouth Hoe, another Hamlet too soon might have been disastrous. None came until March 1926, and this, in a text shorter than the statutory three hours, proved to be a competent recital. Alexander Marsh, in his mid-thirties, was a small, vibrant man with diamond-edged speech that cut an undeviating furrow through the play. Eager to know what could happen, I was unimpressed when it did: the cast remained stereotyped. The Ghost arrived not for any startling disclosure, but to fill a spare quarter of an hour before the glow-worm showed the matin to be near and duly dimmed his ineffectual fire.

Marsh, his own director, had arranged the play in thirteen scenes, short black-outs between each, and two main intervals, though there was little enough to change in the curtains and a few simple sets: the eye of faith had to distinguish between A Room in the Castle, A Hall in the Castle, and A Room of State. Greet's (Darch's) *Hamlet* had been also in thirteen scenes, opening on Ramparts Near the Castle and with no programme-clue to the number of intervals, three, I think (the average length at the Royal was fifteen minutes); Baynton had eighteen scenes, beginning on The Battlements, and with two intervals; and Milton, fourteen scenes and two intervals, A Platform to begin, and frequent returns to a very draughty Room in the Castle.

By Marsh's time, and at seventeen, among a great deal of head-shaking, I had veered to local journalism instead of concentrating on history (the official plan). It occurred to me – here my headmaster, given to acting in the plays of Synge, was mildly sympathetic – that one day drama criticism might emerge. Sooner than I had guessed, it did. The platform-before-the-castle was among a handful of provincial Sunday newspapers, the *Western Independent*, nothing like its successor. Owned by the Astors – Lady Astor followed her husband as Member of Parliament for a Plymouth division – it was controlled by the most regarded editor in Devon and Cornwall, R. A. J. Walling, chief, before amalgamation, of one of two Plymouth dailies, the *Mercury*; J. C. Squire was trained there in the Edwardian daybreak. Walling had as his *Independent* deputy J. J. (James Joseph) Judge, a previous editor of the local *Evening Herald*. Nothing could have been happier for anybody learning how to write about almost everything in a historic provincial city. My trial engagement was a Repertory play, the sentimental *Daddy Longlegs*. The task alarmed me, but by curtain-rise nobody could have known more about the dramatist, Jean Webster (some leagues from *Hamlet*), than I did; though the very site of the theatre is lost, I can still rebuild the place in the mind, even to a diagonal fray across the carpet under the seventh row of stalls. On leaving the seventh row and the matinee I wrote at pedantic length under a tea-shop awning – no time to go inside – and delivered my copy four hours too soon: a record of some kind, and unrepeated. Anyway, the notice did appear, and I got down to genuine work.

Walling, in middle age, was lean and upright under a bush of silver hair; Judge was much shorter, with prominent eyebrows, pebble-glasses, polished apple cheeks and a strongly developed social conscience. He would talk of Shakespeare on occasion, having seen Irving as Iachimo, a collectors' prize he evoked, far from vividly, in quick barks, 'A man – let me say – above – his fellows'. Seldom touching on Shakespeare, Walling gave me an early lesson in drama criticism by warning me never to call anybody or anything 'convincing': 'Meaningless, Mr Trewin,' he said gravely (we were always polite on the *Independent*). 'Read Ivor Brown.' I listened with awe, for R. A. J. was a friend of 'Q.' (Sir Arthur Quiller-Couch) who, if up from Fowey, would drop in at our office: an event when, for half an hour or so, nothing stirred outside the editorial door.

Regretfully, I had other obligations than the theatre: in mid-week, police courts on the Dartmoor fringe; endless interviewing (only a single centenarian); what we knew as Cornish Notes; the desperate tedium of politics, any brand; at winter weekends, Rugby football. Reasonably, I still rescue from the medley the sight of a veteran actress, Dame Madge Kendal, opening a suburban bazaar with regal and terrifying control, everyone with her reduced to irrelevant supers. All of this had nothing to do with *Hamlet*; for years no performance in view. I went on reading about it. Le Mesurier and his family had moved to east Devon; but he left me, as a final Shakespearian bequest, a passage from Dr Johnson that I would quote and re-quote:

> The scenes are interchangeably diversified with merriment and solemnity; with merriment that includes judicious and instructive observations, and solemnity, not strained by poetical violence above the natural sentiments of man. New characters appear from time to time in continual succession, exhibiting various forms of life and particular modes of conversation . . . Every personage produces the effect intended.

(Remembering the most recent Ghost, I was dubious about the last six words.) Father was dimly interested in this; infinitely more when I told him the tragedy had been acted 'after a fish dinner' aboard the East India Company's ship *Dragon*, off Sierra Leone in March 1608. 'Which I permit,' the Captain wrote, 'to keep my people from unlawful games or sleep.' I did assume, from a slight glazing in Father's expressive blue eyes that, professionally, the Captain's action was arguable.

London, I realised, had been having all the luck: no chance there for unlawful games or sleep. During 1925,

when I was at school, the American John Barrymore had
played his forty-three-year-old Hamlet against the Robert
Edmond Jones setting of stairway and vast arch; a Sunday
night society had a solid performance by Godfrey Tearle;
and, most discussed – my headmaster discussed it with
enthusiasm – Barry Jackson, from Birmingham, had put on
a modern dress production, with Colin Keith-Johnston as
the Prince: 'The prose side of the medallion,' a critic said.
Frank Vosper, whose family were from Plympton, near
Plymouth, was a sleek and dangerous King. According to
Hubert Griffith, of the *Observer*, who had a habit of going
to extremes, this was the best Hamlet he had known: 'We
are quite simply at a little modern Catholic court – say
Ruritania, say of a very small Catholic kingdom.' Popu-
larly and maddeningly, it was '*Hamlet* in plus-fours'.

Surely, I assumed, the stage for *Hamlet* (and no debatable
experiment) must be in Stratford-upon-Avon itself. So
with Iris, on a blazing July afternoon in 1929, I reached the
Shakespearian omphalos, as Walling put it in a cherished
'boss word', a Stratford so quiet in those days that visitors
now might not credit the near-pastoral hush. Streets were
uncrowded; you could walk down the middle of the
Warwick Road, look undisturbed at the tomb in Holy
Trinity church, see only an infrequent boat within the
smooth curve of the Avon reach, and spend a morning
alone among the flower patterns in the Knot Garden of
New Place.

At the time there was no Memorial Theatre. The first
(with its tall Romanesque campanile), opened in 1879
through the perseverance of a local idealist, had depended
largely upon the ardour of another idealist, Frank Benson;
between 1886 and 1919, with a few breaks, he had directed
brief annual festivals, bringing his touring company on an
arrangement with the Memorial Governors. A young and
expert Shakespearian, W. Bridges-Adams (whom Ben

Greet had christened, not altogether accurately, 'Un-abridges') succeeded Benson; the theatre moved quietly forward, but on a March afternoon in 1926 it was burned down, nobody knew how. Calm and decisive, Bridges-Adams was ready with a spring season at the local Picture House which had a long, wide auditorium, a raked ground floor, and a variety of lush Venetian panels in watery moonlight; the stage was doubled in size, dressing rooms were added, and for six years, while waiting for a new theatre, the festivals would endure: a month in spring, longer in summer. Only two or three London drama critics bothered to investigate, a gap in record, for Bridges-Adams cared about the speaking of Shakespeare and the simple and flexible staging of the plays.

Stratford, when I went to the Picture House, had in George Hayes a compact and subtle Shakespearian who had won over the Old Vic as Richard II and, remarkably, Aaron in *Titus Andronicus*. He had played Osric and Laertes during Forbes-Robertson's farewell years; suggestions of that classic delivery haunted his own Hamlet, and I had seldom known anyone use fewer gestures. He was at his meridian as Richard II, poignant in lyric grief and the ultimate Pomfret metaphysics. His Hamlet, at forty-one, could be over-explanatory, swift in movement and mind but apt to sacrifice character to grave music. I looked for Ernest Milton's hypnotic passion on a night when he could have said with Eliphaz the Temanite in the *Book of Job*, 'Fear came upon me, and trembling . . . Then a spirit passed before my face; the hair of my flesh stood up.' Hayes had an odd habit of pausing before the last line of any long speech. Still, certain scenes were always lapidary. The tenderness ('Thou art e'en as just a man') of the homage to Horatio lingers yet, and the elegiac-ironic sense of 'Did these bones cost no more than to play at loggats with them?' Bridges-Adams had others to rely upon: the grandly flamboyant

Claudius of Wilfrid Walter, an actor who delighted to act; Eric Maxon (Horatio), his style and panache legacies from years with Beerbohm Tree; the chiselled Polonius, seldom lapsing into buffoonery, of Kenneth Wicksteed, who had played more Shakespearian parts than almost anyone; and a young actress, Joyce Bland's Ophelia, rose of May.

We found ourselves travelling to Stratford every April and July while a new theatre, externally an austere design by Elisabeth Scott, and discussed by Stratford people with brow-wrinkling doubt, was rising behind a wooden fence across the Bancroft meadow. *Hamlet* had left the repertory after 1929. In 1931 a leading man respected in Stratford returned to the festival, as Leontes and Lear; Randle Ayrton was a noble crag of an actor who never worried about London and who spoke with experienced wisdom and the verbal mannerisms ('wăn', 'glăss'), often described as Curzonian. It was round this period that in very minor parts there was an endeared figure, William Calvert, who had appeared at the Memorial in 1881; when he spoke all seemed to pause for a moment in respect.

I had to make do at second hand with news of London Hamlets, again several of them. Of Esme Percy's, at the Royal Court, James Agate said that 'he did not take up arms against his sea of troubles so much as bob up and down upon them like a cork'. Henry Ainley, in some Haymarket performances, was restless and leonine; and at the Old Vic John Gielgud, then twenty-six, received astonishing notices for his lonely Prince, young, unmannered, and beautifully spoken. Before this, when up for a night in 1929, I had caught his Oberon, a shaft of silver, in a partnership with Leslie French's unexampled Puck ('I go, I go; *look* how I go').

IV

The Stratford theatre was to open in 1932. Twelve months

earlier, working with Muriel Day, who lived on the Warwick road and whose experience paralleled mine, I contemplated ambitiously a record of the Memorial Theatre. With Iris's help we finished the book; it was accepted, and we looked for prefaces. Courteously, Bridges-Adams agreed by return. In the summer of 1931 we invited Sir Frank Benson, who in an old age that was most people's youth would be visiting Plymouth in the decline of his touring career; behind him, inevitably, Harold Neilson, not a likeable person, as relentless manager and goad.

For roughly three decades, until 1919, Stratford and Benson had been inseparable names. There, with his company, he had played Hamlet at twenty-seven; he never forgot a warm Easter Monday night when, waiting to go on, he looked from his dressing room window across the riparian silence to the spire of Holy Trinity. Thence he passed into the theatre's history, vague, gentle, long-striding, with a Greek profile and a voice like a crackling fire. 'Poor players, begging friars,' he said, 'we go up and down the land that people may never go without an opportunity of seeing Shakespeare played by a company devoted to his service.' He was scholar and seer, a man who could behave like Quixote and speak with the voice of the Shakespearian kings. Now in early autumn he had walked from Torquay to Plymouth, thirty-seven miles. We saw him at the Royal among its gilt and plush and the meagre stage sets which Edward J. Wood, who acted on the tours, summarised for me as 'Local scenery; our own oak chamber set hung with tapestries; also velvet tabs'. 'Young Hamlet' was seventy-two; his face was medieval work from a carved misericord, but the spirit dwelt in that idealised, abstracted performance, its patrician quality, a slow-moving majesty of gesture ('this brave o'erhanging firmament') admired by Bridges-Adams, the voice, and its long vowels, that could rise in a distant, sometimes semi-liturgical chant. Benson never 'talked' the lines. One of his actors of four years earlier, George Hagan, described to me the 'rather high, floating *legato* tones, particularly in *Hamlet* and *Richard II*. His Hamlet, which he chanted with great beauty and feeling, remains in my head mostly as a musical sound, like the voice of a great singer.' That night he kept us aware of a far-off life re-lived; the company round him (Madge Compton as Ophelia) was affectionately loyal.

On the Saturday afternoon we went down to the theatre early. He was to play Theseus in *A Midsummer Night's Dream* and to be 'discovered' at curtain-rise. With about fifteen minutes to go the stage doorkeeper was habitually calm: 'Don't worry. He'll be running up the street'; and a minute later, at the corner of the building, and between it and the Plymouth Athenaeum, Frank Benson was in sight, running up the slope, hatless, his long dappled hair disordered, and a huddle of books and newspapers under his arm. 'Stratford?' he said, pausing; 'Come round after the play.' He vanished while the doorkeeper shook a forgiving head. After watching his Theseus, gracious and detached, we went back-stage among the dust of years to the dressing room where Benson sat, still wearing the Duke's wreath but looking in repose like a contemplative, ascetic prelate. The introduction? By all means: we must remind him by letter (and we had to, at the twelfth hour). Memory could be deceiving. Only the other afternoon he had come to the wings dressed as Malvolio and found that the play was *The Tempest*. He smiled, musingly and forgivingly. Strange, was it not?

The preface, when it arrived, was Bensonian to the last comma. Though three or four lines were misquoted, we would not have dreamt of altering them. Critics were glum about 'Not in the bulk or the size of a man, but in the heart, Master Page, 'tis here, 'tis here'; but none would mock

Benson's wistful farewell: 'The little rushlight I have carried will soon need snuffing out; perhaps a spark or two may linger for a while in the midst of the flame of the more brilliant beacon.'

I saw him next at Stratford on the following April 23, 1932 – not, alas, when he proposed 'The Immortal Memory' at the Birthday luncheon in a New Place marquee. Here he spoke with so much repetitive eloquence, so many parentheses, so sustained a flight of metaphor that, tactfully, he had to be reminded to let Stanley Baldwin reply before the coming of the Prince of Wales, by air, to open the new theatre. For me Benson's final apotheosis was his appearance as Shylock at a Whit Monday matinee with his old associates round him: a Who's Who from the classical theatre he had known. According to that ancient of days, the Bensonian prompt book, the production first brought together a group of Venetian scenes, then those at Belmont. The fifth act was cut: it would never have done to go on after Shylock's exit from the Trial. The curtain dropped without warning on 'I am not well; send the deed after me / And I will sign it.' When it rose again, Bridges–Adams stepped forward with a laurel chaplet, addressed simply to 'Pa', which he laid at Benson's feet while a new theatre roof just survived the clamour.

V

At home the year was strange. Father, who for months had been writing his memories of a young seaman in the 1870s, died suddenly. In momentary crisis and chaos, none of us seeing how rash it might be, we searched for a house at Stratford with Shakespeare's church and its bells almost in the back garden. This was rash because I knew nothing at all of freelancing, never the easiest sport. Not, for a while, that this disturbed me. I went up for the summer's plays, mostly uncertain in this new splendour; at the back of the stalls we heard somebody from the Picture House audience muttering, 'It's all too *public* here', and I knew what she meant.

Then, before I could join Mother and Iris permanently, I had news that should have made 'each petty artery in the body as hardy as the Nemean lion's nerve'. Walling had talked to his son, secretary of the Institute of Journalists; in my last weeks I heard that the oldest daily newspaper, the *Morning Post* (invariably romantic to me) needed a reporter: nobody guessed that the *Post*, which seemed eternal, was in the last six years of a life that had begun in 1772. I was offered the job. On my twenty-fourth birthday, a stranger in a strange land, out of the *Independent*'s protection (and succeeded by a new female reporter whom one day I would know extremely well), I listened, the first time of many, to the flirting pigeons in Fountain Court and went from the Middle Temple's Tudor Street archway to an office high over the Argus printing works. Among the dozen or twenty people met that foggy morning was the drama critic, S. R. (Robin) Littlewood, rosy, Pickwickian – a perfect resemblance – and ready to talk to an inarticulate stranger about the London theatre. I told him that lately in Plymouth we had had nothing Shakespearian except a visit from Allan Wilkie, who had been for years in Australia, and his leading lady, known as 'Miss Hunter-Watts': her name was Frediswyde. A *Macbeth* was as melancholy as a passing-bell. No *Hamlet* (Wilkie was over fifty). Robin Littlewood nodded with accustomed politeness. 'Hamlet?' he said. 'You'll have missed John Gielgud . . . Ah well, you'll be seeing him again.'

4
TRAGEDIANS OF THE CITY: 1932–36

I

UNDOUBTEDLY I would see Gielgud's Hamlet, as firmly the central performance of its age as Forbes-Robertson's had been: at that hour he had no legitimate rival in the classical theatre. But I would have to wait for nearly two years: a complex interval, especially during 1933 when I was borne on the mill-race of so individual (and lovable) a newspaper as the *Post*. Moreover, before we had settled in north London, I often whisked back to Stratford on the evening train, frequently over-taking Hayes – again with the company – in the warm red brick of Southern Lane as he walked home from the theatre: he lodged next door to us in College Street. If it were a *Macbeth* night he would have his inevitable headache: Theodore Komisarjevsky, the ingenious Russian director, who started during the 1920s, had decided that Macbeth should utter the entire Cauldron scene during an anguished nightmare, and it became anguish for the player, especially anyone of Hayes's charged sensitivity.

In a flash Stratford had altered under the stress of what Bridges-Adams christened the Petrol Age. Most of its swarming visitors came not to see Shakespeare but to stare at the new building; Benson's country retreat, and indeed ours as late as 1929, had irreparably vanished. I thought of a

Lizard recluse at the beginning of a summer season: 'My dear, just step out and there's a dozen round 'ee. *And* they old motors!'

I chanced to be at home when the 'Gower' Shakespeare Monument was moved. It had stood behind the theatre since a late-Victorian autumn. Now the governors had given it to the town, and the town had taken it to a commanding site – if still with its back to the theatre – by the grey medieval thrust of Clopton Bridge. In Lord Ronald Gower's elaborate memorial Shakespeare was seated on a high circular plinth upon a pedestal, and one of four life-sized bronzes round the pedestal was Hamlet with the skull: 'Prince Hamlet, green as a penny, heaved a bronze sigh,' wrote the Cornish poet, Charles Causley. There would be a fresh performance in the theatre that September, nothing for *Hamlet* history ('operatic' said Bridges-Adams philosophically years later) but cast by popular demand after the same player had triumphed as Coriolanus in the spring. A stunningly handsome romantic extrovert, Anew McMaster was the brother-in-law of a finer artist, Micheál MacLiammóir, and worked mainly in the Irish 'smalls' where he was greatly admired. There could have been few actors less like Hamlet, certainly not the 'Gower' Hamlet, than this florid technician, who did achieve dignity now and again, but who turned the new theatre, all steel and marble and mahogany, into a private barn and stormed it happily. One could not be too dismayed, for Hamlet was having an expansively good time, even if he would never have hesitated about anything in his life and found events at Elsinore inexplicable. Throwing off the speeches confidently, he would have liked, I felt – had it been conceivable – to have added the First Player's as a bonus. The night was vigorously uncomplicated, an impression reaffirmed when McMaster returned to the part that winter, with slighter means and a cast of his own – some

Stratfordians in it – at the Chiswick Empire. There, or at Stratford, but not from him, I heard a grandly comprehensive spoonerism, 'So frowned he once when, in an angry parle, he sled the smoted loopacks on the ice.' Such an oddity as this, wormwood to the academic, can preserve some lesser production in the mind; but we had nothing in those days like a passing thought of Frank Benson, years before, that he put into practice and persevered with: he allowed Hamlet, back from his voyage, to enter dressed in blue and bearing a fishing net with which to catch the conscience of the King.

Late in 1933 I had in the West End of London one of those minor experiences that can establish themselves indelibly. It was at the Lyric Theatre, Shaftesbury Avenue, during a play by a respected American professor, Talbot Jennings; its principal figure Shakespeare himself, acted by Leslie Howard. We know, alas, that little can be as dead as a stage biography of Shakespeare. *This Side Idolatry*, less embarrassing than most, included a Globe Theatre rehearsal of *Hamlet* that had judgment and reason on its side and illuminated a text otherwise shadowy. Though it expired after ten days, the last audience rose and cheered; when this happens there must be a cause that critics have not spied. It was not solely Howard's expertise and tact: his cast in general seemed to share a belief in the proceedings. But what I remember now is an extraordinary half minute – the epithet is weighed – when the boy player of Ophelia, Peter Spagnioletti, of whom I had never heard or would again, spoke in his clear treble, 'And I of ladies most deject and wretched' with a beauty as affecting as lark-song. Time has not obscured that Ophelia; I doubt that it will.

II

At last, in November 1934, I was in the New Theatre (the

Albery today) eager for Hamlet to declare himself, and oblivious of those who said, a familiar reaction, that I should have seen the form and feature of blown youth at the Old Vic years before. Gielgud was still only thirty, Hamlet's age according to the Gravedigger, a detail that has tormented editors rather than listeners: 'I came to't that day . . . that young Hamlet was born . . . I have been sexton here, man and boy, thirty years.' To go to the play with any kind of preconception is dangerous; still, I knew what Gielgud's voice should be: it would have been absurd to question his intelligence as an actor. A Terry, deriving from the royal family of the stage, 'bred-up with eagle-birds of Jove', his princeliness was obvious. One waited for the voice, ever the hardest quality to define. Shaw said of Forbes-Robertson's that it resembled 'the chalumeau register of the clarionet', not perhaps the immediate phrase in a listener's mind. Gielgud's voice had been likened to the oboe, the Elizabethan hautboy. As I heard it that night, it had the range of a violin, a Stradivarius controlled by a master. This was the ultimate music of the word, sound and sense in unison. Fastidiously scored, lofty in spirit, it had to be, in pace, breeding, emotion, and the suppleness of what the nineteenth century called 'transitions', the classic Hamlet that audiences of the time expected; I could not have wished to see and hear more clearly what the American critic, Rosamond Gilder, would describe as 'the prototype of all lost and lonely souls'. If a few passages – the Ghost scene was one – did not excite me with Milton's heart-stopping power, Gielgud animated for me Matthew Arnold's phrase about Man being viewed as balancing and indeterminate, swayed by a thousand subtle influences, physiological and pathological. Hamlet is agonisingly sensitive and disillusioned; the duty of revenge terrifies him; elaborately he argues through the ratiocinative soliloquies, seeking confirmation for what is too surely confirmed. His purpose is 'almost blunted'; when at last he strikes, his own life is lost.

Back at the Theatre Royal, just a decade before, they would have wondered at the permanent set (by a designer known as Motley) for fourteen scenes that accommodated one interval of twelve minutes. It was placed upon a turntable, with a cyclorama for the exteriors and for the last scene against the sky; to suggest the interiors, long painted canvas curtains, swagged and draped, and patterned in silver and blue. Costumes (with a 'rich, worn look' said Gielgud), and inspired by Dürer's contemporary, Lucas Cranach, were of silk- and velvet-trimmed canvas and sprayed with autumnal colour. This is factual: my immediate impression was of the corrupt court of Elsinore in thunder-light, waiting for the onset of a tumultuous storm and, through all, the sound of that questing violin. Claudius (Frank Vosper) and Gertrude (Laura Cowie) seem now to have been larger than life; Jessica Tandy's Ophelia could not have been more touching in bewildered grief; and George Howe poised his Polonius between shrewdness and a blurring garrulity: in a Gielgud invention the old man was stabbed through the arras by the sword that Hamlet had stolen earlier during the King's prayer. Throughout (and Fortinbras was there at the last) it was a night textually ample, untortured and veracious. Gielgud has said that, in studying a speech, he is 'aware of the whole span of the arc, the beginning, middle, and end of the passage'; and that, too, describes his method of production. We realised at the New that Hamlet's advice to the Players came from the director's heart.

III

Those early London years would be the most demanding in my life away from the theatre. Besides doing anything that turned up, and the *Post* newsroom ensured that a great deal did, I was primarily a descriptive writer: watchful at ceremonies in the Abbey or St Paul's, seeing medieval colour renewed in a cathedral's monastic cloisters, or listening to Scots fishwives singing to the King and Queen on a quay by the Firth of Forth. A sterner task was to go round what at the peak of unemployment were known as the depressed areas: hearing the silence of the Tyne, threading rain-blotted slag-heaps in mining Durham, talking to listless groups in the street of dismantled Haltwhistle, or in a land behind the ranges in west Cumberland, and being shown through a long day the desert of the Rhondda. Those were grim weeks: selfishly, in escapist London, it was happier to be acknowledged as understudy to Robin Littlewood: not that I could be in any sense a replacement for that inimitable man as he returned from the newest première: the bustling entry into a corner of the reporters' room; adjustments of a chair; intricate business with a programme lost among several strata of envelopes; the insertion into the typewriter of a sheet of paper, and its instant removal; an act-by-act summary of the night's events for anybody who happened to be in the room; and at length, while sub-editors peered in anxiously, the beginning of the notice, punctuated by encouraging comments to himself: 'Good, Littlewood, good!', or 'You're in form tonight, Littlewood!', or, more rarely, 'No, *no*, Littlewood! Not like that at all!'

He was irreplaceable; but I deputised for him often, once at a curious Old Vic performance of *Antony and Cleopatra* during the autumn of 1934. In the auditorium and a coffee-flavoured underworld, these premières were like exclusive club nights; Miss Baylis presided in her box, and people from gallery to stalls knew each other, the play's record at the Vic, and its companies (said the critic Lionel Hale) since an unfortunate transference to the Ark. On this occasion

Mary Newcombe, always a competent actress, could reach Cleopatra; her Antony, perversely miscast, was Wilfrid Lawson, sometimes an inspired character-man but now, with a gold wreath slipping over one eye, and a slurred, throaty delivery, next to inaudible in mid-stalls. A partisan gallery, ignoring him, shouted incessantly for 'Caesar'!' as to a new idol. This was the Octavius, Maurice Evans, who would be for months the *Victor ludorum* of Waterloo Road. Though he looked like a possible athlete, and presently a Richard II who could have opened the batting, his burnished speech had the lyric passion, the intellectual intensity, the sharp definition, that soon New York would applaud. Next spring Evans's Old Vic Hamlet (he was thirty-three), in the 'eternity' version, first I had known, could not approach his Richard: it was a confident, controlled portrait of somebody who was passing through Elsinore and had resolved in friendly fashion to keep us abreast of what was going on: no mystification or pot-shots at a phrase. It puzzled me why this sensible personage behaved as he did to Ophelia, Vivienne Bennett, an actress of exquisite repose who did not treat the Mad scene like a dislodged fragment of ballet.

No contemporary actor in the mid-1930s was any rival to Gielgud, whose Hamlet remained for 155 performances at the New. During June 1935 Michéal MacLiammóir led the Dublin Gate company at the Westminster in a production by Hilton Edwards, a strong and baleful Claudius. While recognising the atmospheric décor and lighting – particularly the lighting – I could not believe that Hamlet did more than exhibit his power of rhetorical attack. In coming years we would greet MacLiammóir, an actor with a witty fold in the voice and abundant resilience on stage and off, but *Hamlet* that June melted like a summer cloud and, with it, the customary and ignored key questions. Today I ask in vain whether Edwards's King saw the dumbshow, or whether indeed there was a dumbshow to be seen.

IV

The *Post* appeared to go serenely forward. Without embarrassing self-consciousness it kept its tradition of lucid writing and independent thought. Such men as H. A. Gwynne (the veteran editor), Ian Colvin, and Robert Hield observed their juniors benevolently, and these, if pretending to be amused by *Post* politics, a steady Right-wheel, were unwaveringly loyal, Horatios to a man. During 1936 outer events had darkened. In Britain it was the contentious reign of Edward VIII. Abroad the Nazis loomed, and I saw some of their frightening regimentation when going for a month to the Olympic Games in a Berlin heavy with the swastika, a study in scarlet. These were the Games at which Jesse Owens, the black runner (whom Hitler disdained) looked, as he won the 200 metres, like a master in charge of schoolboys. Away from the stadium, and in the city's repellent cynicism, I had hoped to find a *Hamlet* as relief: none in any theatre, but in the Schauspielhaus I discovered Werner Krauss's Lear striking the map asunder with his sword ('Cornwall and Albany, with my two daughters' dowers, digest this third'). It was a night of power without glory, in the tone of the period a disciplined military manoeuvre.

At home the year had two *Hamlets*, a first in the gilt casket of the Lyric Theatre at Hammersmith. There an actor of a very old school, Arthur Phillips, presented himself indulgently in all the major parts (before Hamlet he had been Shylock, Richard II, Macbeth, and the Mephistopheles of Göethe's *Faust*). His place, as Baynton's used to be, was the dead centre of the stage. Nobody would have grudged him his fun, even if, as the productions followed each other, muscle-bound, I did recall a Cornish local preacher at odds with Shadrach, Meshach and Abednego. At the fourth return of 'Cornet, flute, harp, sackbut, psaltery and dulcimer' he said to his congregation, 'You do know what I mean, brethren – band as before.' Phillips' Hamlet, who must have been over fifty and a tetchy companion at Wittenberg, was a deliberate, high-pitched speaker who seemed to be multiplying the syllables, manufacturing his own echoes. He had with him some players easier to listen to, Dorothy Holmes-Gore for one, and Basil Gill who doubled the Ghost with a Fortinbras (anonymous in the programme) of a Viking splendour that might have satisfied Bridges-Adams.

We continued to go down to Stratford, though wistfulness kept breaking in: the new theatre's stage could seem tiresomely remote ('like playing from Folkestone to Boulogne' said the actor Baliol Holloway). Bridges-Adams had resigned – an idealist frustrated by the chairman of his governors whose notions were drearily dogmatic – and his place was taken from 1935 by Ben Iden Payne, a mildly obsessed scholar and a disciple of the neo-Elizabethan William Poel. Payne had spent so long in America that his name was scarcely remembered: unfairly because, working for the founder of the British repertory movement, Miss Horniman, in Manchester, he had been among the main pillars of that cause. Not that this made him a good choice for Stratford, averse as he was from 'scenic investiture' (his own phrase) and given to a low-keyed form of Elizabethan production that, in his contrivance, seldom stirred the blood. After seven years he would leave so quietly that playgoers, with other things to worry them in the middle of the war, hardly knew that he had gone. Stratford during much of the thirties meant the latest piece of agreeable impertinence by Theodore Komisarjevsky. Bridges-Adams had introduced him to the festivals; until 1939 he was there practically every year, his productions capricious, wildly and pictorially inventive, finding genuine tragedy in his staircase-*Lear*, and expressing always a theatrical zest that Stratford needed and the amiable Iden Payne could not conceive.

Payne had to depend more than commonly upon his casting at a day when the Memorial standard had perilously slumped, and during 1936 he had three players untouched by mediocrity: the veteran Randle Ayrton, a Lear for Komisarjevsky's storm; a young man who was climbing fast and with an enviable stamina, Donald Wolfit; and an actress at seventeen, Pamela Brown, promising already what she would fulfil and looking wide-eyed into the future as she lisped 'A woeful Cwessid 'mongst the mewwy Gweeks!' That autumn Payne directed Hamlet for Wolfit, then thirty-four and playing in décor dominated mainly by a huge rear window. He had been a Shakespearian in the Doran company (Aguecheek at Plymouth Theatre Royal), had acted in taxing repertory seasons, won the Old Vic audience for a group of parts that included a scorching Claudius to Gielgud's Hamlet, and kept consistently at work. Suddenly, in effect, Stratford was his.

On his Hamlet night, he recalled, Ayrton, as generous as crotchety, looked over his shoulder in the dressing room mirror and said, 'Give them a bit of the old.' Wolfit did (taking such an instruction as Payne's to rush over during the Play scene to distract the King from the dumbshow). Burly and, a critic said, 'bourgeois', unused to the princely rituals of Elsinore, he contrived to romanticise his aspect; certainly he developed the part from the first soliloquy with a swelling emotion that never let the audience sag. It seemed almost that Wolfit, aware that Hamlet was in deadly danger, wanted to know (and his listeners did) what would happen next; night by night he thought himself afresh into the part. We had to take grace for granted: this was a living, passionate man, fighting with the world and himself, as indeed Wolfit would fight during most of his stage career. The taut, powerful voice had not yet begun to repeat its cadences: this early Hamlet was the statement of an actor giving them 'a bit of the old', his intention, undiminished, through life.

5
AFFAIR AT ELSINORE:
1937–39

I

AT the beginning of 1937 Laurence Olivier joined the Old Vic to play Hamlet, Sir Toby Belch, and Henry V under the direction of Tyrone Guthrie. Twenty-nine years old, eloquent in panache and vitality, with Italianate good looks and a strongly-wrought theatrical imagination, he had been spoken of as challenging Gielgud: 'the usurper,' said a critic sourly, as if that kind of comparison could be at all valid: it came up simply because, at Gielgud's suggestion, the men had alternated Romeo and Mercutio during a famous season at the New. Though Olivier's Romeo entered direct from the high Renaissance, everyone except the critic St John Ervine, who followed no kind of fashion, told him frigidly that he was not a verse-speaker: why go on? Disbelieving, he resolved to play himself into Shakespeare. Hence his arrival in Waterloo Road, and in time his fortune to be the first Hamlet on the sacred ground of Elsinore, the castle of Kronborg itself. Never palely loitering behind the arches of the years, Olivier would have been renowned at court for his physical accomplishments, long held irrelevant to a picture of melancholy and despair.

So we saw him that chill January at the Vic. The occasion tempted me, whenever possible – and luck did survive – to get away early from the Tudor Street corridor, slip over Blackfriars Bridge, and by courtesy of an already-loved figure, Mrs Clark of the box office, to meet Iris in the sixth or seventh row of the stalls. On stage those nights were possibly the most athletic in classical record. Tyrone Guthrie, observant heron of a man (I could almost have imagined him standing, one-legged, in the tide of Helford River), had no objection to the chasing and leaping: for him anything relishingly theatrical could be excused. But he, and Olivier after him, had also been possessed by Freudian theory which its high priest, the psychiatrist, Dr Ernest Jones, considered infallible. In *Hamlet*, apparently, it was a matter of the Oedipus complex: everyone, I gathered too late and without enthusiasm, should have known it from the moment when Hamlet, in the opening line of his first soliloquy, turned 'solid' to 'sullied' – 'O that this too, too *sullied* flesh would melt' – and angrily wiped from his face his mother's kiss. Other hints must have proliferated: to no purpose, for hardly anybody noticed them. Much anxious thinking went to waste, though years ahead both Guthrie and Olivier were still remembering the Freudian idea. Ivor Brown (in a book that I edited) would say, though not of the Guthrie productions: 'Does hesitation to murder need all the argle-bargle that the professors have bestowed on the psychology of Hamlet?'

What did matter was the night's unrelaxed excitement in the full text and in a setting, a composition of steps and platforms that must have been planned simply to make things more difficult. The company had to be in training as the action whirled about: I recall with awe the Queen's backward dying fall from a height, waiting to be fielded – and mercifully she was – by an anxious group below.

In Olivier we had less the Hamlet of indecision than the flash and outbreak of a fiery mind. Night by night, stamina unwavering, he sprang across the set, rostrum upon rostrum, to a breaking surf of Old Vic cheers: the gallery, which could be fairly critical, was never in any doubt that this was the Hamlet it wished to see. Today, though my own memories are principally visual, one speech is inseparable from the mosaic-*Hamlet* that through the decades becomes definitive in the mind. I mean that emphatic cry, half-wailed, half-proclaimed, the mounting desperation of 'I do not know / Why yet I live to say "This thing's to do." ' Other performers fuelled the excitement: Francis Sullivan's gross King and an animated rapier of a Laertes by Michael Redgrave, himself a Hamlet to be. We learned too from Alec Guinness's Reynaldo – Guinness was another Hamlet on the way – what character could emerge from a few curt speeches. We had bothered too little about this Reynaldo from the household of Polonius, a trusted servant sent to Paris to keep an eye on Laertes and – in the peculiarly roundabout way Polonius prescribed – to discover what he could. Here the old man is particularly dithering and inconsecutive: I can see Reynaldo as he listened with a discreet, hooded smile to his master's haverings and found a gentle emphasis for his reply to 'You have me, have you not?' – 'My lord, I *have.*' There was a much smaller success that night, the composite man-around-Elsinore (acted by Crichton Stuart) that Guthrie labelled simply 'Messenger'. Given the Gentleman's 'Save yourself, my lord' before the entry of Laertes, he spoke it with so much fire that Charles Morgan awarded him a special note in *The Times* review.

It was Coronation year, so on an early morning in May I came up from Kensington where we were living then and climbed to the press seats in the triforium of Westminster Abbey: immediately below was the ceremonial platform called the Theatre, 'a stage . . . set up four-square at the crossing of the Transepts' and spread with a carpet of gold that held and stored the light. During the afternoon I was back in Tudor Street for the most concentrated four hours' work I remember, an attempt to get on paper a coherent idea of the ceremonial, its significances, its colours and its sounds. That returns to me now, the sight of the Archbishop poising Saint Edward's crown above the anointed, robed and sceptred King, and, later, of the King as he sat enthroned during the Queen's crowning, rigid, motionless, his sceptre held before him, a vision of another monarch from the first year of the minster among the marshes.

Very soon after this I heard that the Danish Tourist Board had invited the Old Vic company to play at the castle of Kronborg, Hamlet's castle. When the news editor said: 'This business at Elsinore. Do you want to go?' I answered fervently, 'Yes', and that evening read Drinkwater's sonnet with its insistence:

> That in all kingdoms now, for ever more,
> Hourly the play begins at Elsinore.

II

From London half a dozen critics and journalists travelled to Elsinore: my sister Iris was with me and that evening, when we boarded the boat at Harwich, we met Ivor Brown, of the *Observer*, least loquacious of men, whom one day I was to know far better, and George Bishop, theatre correspondent of the *Telegraph*, who knew everyone already. Disembarking at the port of Esbjerg on the west coast of Jutland, we went by train through a tranquil world in its summer flowering, and across the islands of Denmark to the peace and cordiality of Copenhagen. My father would say it was the friendliest port he had known (and what did Shakespeare know about it? A good question). Certainly it was welcoming on this late-May night when everybody in the hotel, manager to chambermaids, wanted to hear just what would happen at Elsinore and hastened to remind us of Shakespearian performances we had never met. How would the English play compare with the unorthodox Jensen version just seen in the city, and would it still be Shakespeare's? On reflection we thought it would. Politely, someone called us English ambassadors, which prompted Ivor Brown, always exact, to murmur that in *Hamlet* these existed only to report that Rosencrantz and Guildenstern were dead. 'Where should we have our thanks?'

Next morning, forty miles up the coast, we were at the little town of Helsingör, opposite the Swedish Hälsingborg on the narrowest passage of the Sound. All was shadowed by the vast rose-red castle of Kronborg, its spires and gables and steeply-pitched roofs of weathered green copper above the honeycombed stones and the turreted and flagged courtyard, its walls at least a foot thick. Here Guthrie had been at pains, after a local preliminary error, to reproduce before the northern wall, pierced with many windows, the stage setting used at the Old Vic; the rostrum was there – it may even have been higher – from which Dorothy Dix, the Queen, had to make her dying fall of fifteen feet.

Unluckily, the weather was not looking with a friendly eye on Denmark; rain had been torrential during recent nights, and it appeared that the first British company to visit Kronborg since the late sixteenth century (with the comedian Will Kempe) might be thoroughly unfortunate. Nobody we spoke to, and most people were testing their English, would dream of such a thing; but the Old Vic players, who had been rehearsing in the rain every night (they had to do this because the castle was open to visitors during the day) were much less sanguine. Conditions had been odd. By day the company could admire lilac and laburnum and, as Guthrie said, play tennis or go boating on the Sound. At night, before and during rehearsal, the weather would break. Nobody, gazing towards Sweden, had noticed any 'high eastward hill' over which Horatio saw the morn, in russet mantle clad, though it was agreed that Shakespeare must have his licence. (Years later, Martin Holmes, in *The Guns of Elsinore*, would refer to a print in the *Civitates Orbis Terrarum*, an atlas well-known in the late sixteenth century. Here 'the palace of "Elsenor" stands within a high and massive curtain wall that appears to tower over the sea, while across the strait, hard by the eastern margin of the picture, the coast is seen rising sharply from the water and giving the impression of still greater heights immediately beyond.')

III

The morning of June 2 was depressing. Several times, during a six-hour rehearsal until early in the afternoon, squalls whipped across the Sound: players (permitted now to use the courtyard) were soaked in their overcoats and mackintoshes, and a frigid north wind did nothing to help. Still, the company and the military cadets Guthrie was rehearsing as supers, a towering six-foot-five in his wet mackintosh, remained moderately hopeful. Only moderately. When, holding an umbrella, John Abbott – who had succeeded Sullivan as Claudius – put intense feeling into the line, 'Is there not rain enough in the sweet heavens?' the small and privileged audience, sheltered by an archway, could not forbear to cheer. George Bishop quoted the right line when a sparrow settled, it seemed permanently, on the shoulder of the Ghost (Torin Thatcher): 'There is special providence in the fall of a sparrow.'

Providence was not available that afternoon. A cloudburst saturated the stage and the courtyard benches which should have held 2,500 people; next, a full gale stormed the Sound. An open air production (it would have been

Guthrie's first) was clearly impossible, even though it was supposed to be a gala occasion, with royalty present and the diplomatic corps. About an hour before the play should have begun at eight o'clock, I found myself, not knowing why, standing by Lilian Baylis at the door of the Marienlyst Hotel, half a mile from Kronborg. Huddled into a thick black coat, Miss Baylis was staring at the sky so angrily that I felt she might be shaking her fist at it. Realising that someone was by her, she turned autocratically – and I saw then what an autocrat she was – pointed out to the streaming rain, and said: 'Look, this must stop!' I agreed, but felt, for an awful moment, that I might have been responsible for the whole affair, not forgetting the special trains that by then would have been leaving Copenhagen. While I tried to frame a suitable apology, Tyrone Guthrie came out into the hall, rubbing his hands, and (as he was inclined to do in an emergency) looking surprisingly pleased. 'Going to do it *here*' he said.

'*Here*?' Miss Baylis exclaimed in the kind of italics that Edith Evans would use for Lady Bracknell's 'A *handbag*!'

'Yes,' Guthrie repeated calmly. 'Here.' As he turned, she looked after him in utter bewilderment before pursuing him into the hotel depths.

Guthrie's intended theatre was the hotel ballroom, large, flamboyant, quite unsuitable, but, as George Bishop put it, with no other booking. Beyond its range of windows mist was so dense, obscuring the line of the Swedish coast, that we might have been poised on an unmapped height. The ballroom had only a tiny cabaret stage approached by a short stair and holding a potted palm which Guthrie loved though I have no idea whether it remained. The room had stacks of what Guthrie remembered as basket-chairs but that I think of now as small and not too well-balanced gilt ones. The plan was to present the play more or less in what before long would be called 'the round', a term unknown at that period, with the audience, members, as it were, of the Court, on three sides of the cabaret stage. Promptly Guthrie enlisted the press party which had swollen to include correspondents from several parts of Europe. 'Done nothing yet!' he said; and for the next twenty minutes we did something, organised by Guthrie and his stage manager, to set the chairs in a wide arc and to turn the place into a vague semblance of a theatre. I was paired with a Danish writer who regarded the whole business as peculiar and at heart, I believe, suspected the storm to be a British stage effect.

Outside, waves were riding high in the narrow water between Denmark and Sweden, and it was plain that the storm had set in for the night, with a noise like the ride of the Valkyries. All the costumes and properties had been brought over from Kronborg; hotel bedrooms became dressing rooms; and not so long after eight o'clock the ballroom, with Danish royalty (Prince Knud and Princess Caroline Mathilde) in the front row, was filled for what, in effect, would be an improvisation. It had been left to the players, directed by Laurence Olivier whom Guthrie had put, wisely, in command, to get the night together with only the sketchiest idea of ways and means. We learned afterwards that one door, tightly closed, could not be used because a bird was nesting above it and must by no means be disturbed. Guthrie came forward to apologise briefly for 'the strangest performance of *Hamlet* on any stage', and presently Francisco and Barnardo were on 'the platform before the castle', Horatio and Marcellus were on their way up through the audience, and somewhere, within a few moments, a bell was beating one.

The company rallied with astonishing ease (heroes all of them, Olivier said), as if a group of strolling players had materialised from nowhere, resolved to let fly. Through much of the night those of us who had seen the play at the

Vic wondered what might go wrong during the next minutes. Nothing that mattered did. Olivier, denied his athletics, had not been a surer Hamlet in grace and sympathy; we saw that the new young actress, Vivien Leigh, who had joined the cast as Ophelia, was acting with unflurried spirit. I recall, too, how expertly Torin Thatcher controlled the Ghost during a sustained gale that, battering against the windows, accompanied most of his speech until the glow-worm showed the matin to be near. Lilian Baylis, in cap and gown and with a benevolent gleam in her eye, at first stood at the back. Not for long. She moved to her proper place in the front row, and at the end was seen to be standing, as everybody was, to applaud her company.

By morning the storm had blown itself out. No need to repeat the ballroom performance, though Guthrie must have been wistful – he was never again in love with a normal proscenium stage. On the night of June 3, in the fading of a white-and-blue northern day exquisite in freshness and clarity, everything visible on the Swedish coast except a high, eastward hill, Hamlet spoke at last on the Kronborg platform; swans glimmering in the reedy moat; no other sound but the sighing of the tide. Excitement was there, especially after the Play scene, the King's downward rush through frightened spectators and Hamlet springing for a moment in triumph upon the peak of the stage. But it was not such an event as Danish papers had called 'the night of the ballroom'. Guthrie agreed. The Marienlyst improvisation, he would say nearly a quarter of a century later, had scenes that 'related the audience to *Hamlet* in a different and, I thought, more logical, satisfactory and effective way than can ever be achieved in a theatre of what is still regarded as orthodox design.' Ivor Brown, writing for *Theatre Arts Monthly* not long after Elsinore, put it in his own way: '*Hamlet* "on the very spot" became, except for the coldness of the night air, which true to the text, bit shrewdly, very like *Hamlet* in a modern theatre, whereas *Hamlet* in a ballroom had been strange and different and perhaps more truly Elizabethan.'

IV

A London *Hamlet* we returned to after a lapse of only half-a-dozen weeks had little of the Marienlyst excitement. One could usually count on a demanding production at the Westminster Theatre in Palace Street, a reserved, discreet building that occasionally, I felt, dared an audience to express its enthusiasm. Michael MacOwan, a highly intelligent director, proposed to confine himself to 'the resources of the Globe Theatre company, a sceneless stage, absence of lighting effects, a small company with a limited number of supernumeraries'. This established, he would express the various theories of Professor Dover Wilson that were currently themes for Shakespearian debate: most notably that, before the Nunnery scene, Hamlet should overhear Polonius's suggestion to the King to 'loose my daughter to him' and eavesdrop on what would follow. The night had an austere, barebones quality in practically full lighting throughout and in a formal set designed by Peter Goffin, a gentle artist whom I knew in Plymouth where he was likely to hold you up on a traffic island and invite you to hear satirical poems in the attic-studio he called Endymion. The Westminster Hamlet, Christopher Oldham, stage name of Christopher Scaife, was a donnish anti-romantic, ably spoken without persuading one that he had ever thought the part exciting in the theatre. Two performances linger. Cecil Trouncer (Polonius), in the style that he would progressively heighten, carved out his phrases with the precision of a Grinling Gibbons in leaf and flower. Mark Dignam's Ghost, in unlikely surroundings, was ineffably sepulchral, more so, I imagine, than a German actor

Harcourt Williams once saw as 'an angry old gentleman dressed in a winding-sheet which he manipulated with much fervour, and even thumped his tombstone'. Dignam did not need the accessories.

Down in a still over-crowded and jostling Stratford, and in its slowly maturing theatre, Donald Wolfit had repeated his Hamlet from the previous year (with the huge window, designed by Randle Ayrton, as the background of the principal set). Not many could have complained of Shakespearian tedium or the lack of any sense of occasion. If secondary players were no more than secondary, and by then we had grown accustomed to this, Wolfit, without gain in grace but much in vigorous exposition that drove the play forward, had acted himself deeply into Hamlet. He would explore even further when he took his own company on tour that autumn: prelude to a score of actor-managerial years. He was dominant especially in the soliloquies – in particular the full-pitch attack of 'O, what a rogue and peasant slave!' – which stirred him more than what a Stratford visitor was heard to dismiss as Hamlet's small-talk: not that the technician in Wolfit faltered there.

For me the late summer and early autumn of 1937 were calamitous. Wrongly, I had not troubled about newspaper politics, even when we heard during the summer that Lord Camrose had bought the *Post* and 'would in due course make an announcement of his policy and intentions'. That was probably ominous; and yet it came as a desperate shock when on the afternoon of September 30, with all going mildly according to plan, we were summoned to the sub-editors' room, the biggest in the office. (I can see now the shape of the papers strewn over my desk, and an open book beside the typewriter.) In retrospect I suppose the meeting was a highly theatrical event: in fiction it might have been, but it came through as a painful improvisation where everybody tried, unsuccessfully, to cheer his neighbour (a few could afford it; the majority could not). H. A. Gwynne announced with no kind of histrionics – always against his temperament – that the night's paper would be the last in the *Morning Post*'s history of 165 years: it had been amalgamated with the *Daily Telegraph*. Some of the editorial staff would go up the road to Fleet Street; for others it must be a new beginning.

That night, when Littlewood arrived to write his final review, it was of a play entitled *The Last Straw* (Comedy Theatre) which sounded all too symbolic. For the reporters the *Post* had to die at a feverish supper party at the public house across the street by the Temple gateway: a wake dragged out as long as possible. We parted in ones and twos, swearing to meet very soon, but knowing it to be unlikely.

At home six weeks later there was a grimmer family blow. Iris collapsed suddenly and within minutes had died.

v

For a long time I would be, in Rodney Harmer's words (and his keeping), a permanent freelance at the *Observer* in the calm, blue-curtained building with the projecting clock on the other side of Tudor Street. Harmer, formerly chief sub-editor of the *Post*, was now J. L. Garvin's news editor and in entire charge, subject only to an insistent voice on the telephone: 'the Chief' never arrived from Beaconsfield, but weekly Harmer found work for me from an overflowing and generous invention.

When I went next to *Hamlet* in the autumn of 1938 it was with the former Wendy Monk who had succeeded me on the *Western Independent* six years before: we had just been married at the Devon village church of Tamerton Foliot.

It was a dire period for the provincial stage. Touring companies had all but petered out. (Plymouth, through

City Council dreariness, had lost the Royal, torn down and replaced by a matter-of-fact cinema.) More than ever the British theatre depended upon London, and the classical theatre upon the Old Vic. Lilian Baylis had died late in 1937, her influence bequeathed to Guthrie. He directed the newest Hamlet, Alec Guinness, only twenty-four, who had been Gielgud's Osric and had played both this and Reynaldo with Olivier at Elsinore. (Remarkably, at that age, he had also been 'Uncle Exeter' to Olivier's Henry V at the Vic.) *Hamlet* kept a tingling vitality that the Westminster performances had totally lacked. 'Modern dress I do not greatly care for' said the young Guthrie in 1933; but here, in an 'eternity' text, nearly five hours of it, he translated the play to a Ruritanian setting, Hamlet brought pictorially into the saga of Hentzau and Zenda and the Rassendylls. As a rule, Roger Furse's costumes preferred a formality of Court uniform for the men (Andrew Cruickshank as the King with a chestful of Orders) and long dresses for the women (Veronica Turleigh as the Queen); the atmosphere of some Palace levée. Guinness did enter the graveyard, from his voyage, in a sailor's jersey and thigh-boots. Not that costumes were all-important, or Guthrie's few flourishes of production: the most memorable was the funeral on a very wet day – possibly a recollection of Elsinore weather – the mourners under a grove of open umbrellas.

Guinness was the youngest, quietest Hamlet I had known; an old farm-neighbour would have labelled him as 'a thinking man'. He had a sure pathos and no clamour of staginess for its own sake; he was, too, the first Hamlet, sitting alone by the Players' property basket before 'the conscience of the King', who found himself tapping out the rhythm upon the upturned drum. As he would so often, he seemed to be creating a character as he moved, without previous calculation. The critic and Shakespearian actor,

Robert Speaight, who frequently talked of him, described the performance as 'sensitive and *intimiste*, spurning spectacular effects'. That could not have been more truthful: Guthrie knew his man.

The Munich interregnum almost over, Europe passed inevitably towards war. Yet at the end of June, with the stage behaving as if nothing were wrong, Gielgud took a new *Hamlet*, his third, to the Lyceum Theatre for six performances before he travelled with his company to Elsinore. It was the Lyceum's last play for many years. Though all that survived of Irving's house were the great pillared portico at the foot of Wellington Street and a fragment of rear wall, the name – in spite of decades of melodrama and pantomime – belonged to history, and Gielgud honoured everything the name implied: his *Hamlet* said farewell to a vanished world. He used his Kronborg scenery with its outer and inner stages on a raised platform. Following the published ideas of Granville-Barker, his mentor, who had also advised him after a special rehearsal, he had not acted with more certainty, anguish, or extreme tension, a complete knowledge of the man and his music. Agate captured the feeling of the death scene in which the man really did die, 'as distinct from the star actor who desists'.

It was a night of classical virtuosity. With Gielgud in a poet's 'high lament of summer lost in wrack, a noble nature in its June betrayed', was Fay Compton, an Ophelia never adrift in a Mad Margaret haze. During 1874 her aunt, Isabel Bateman, had been Ophelia to Irving's first Lyceum Hamlet, just as in 1878 Ellen Terry, Gielgud's great-aunt, was Ophelia in the production with which Irving inaugurated his management of the theatre, then the Royal Lyceum. Now Gielgud's epilogue, two months before the war, would be right royal.

6

THROUGH THE WAR:
1939–45

WAR had to come: then, after a year, the apocalyptic fury of the Blitz. The West End stage recovered gradually; Donald Wolfit, as resident actor-manager, battled on against what the novelist M. P. Shiel, in another context, called 'the scoriac tempests of hell'. A prolonged repertory sequence at the Strand Theatre included a Hamlet knowing his mid-stage place and even more passionate than he had been at the Stratford première, which seemed a lifetime away but was only five years. True, it continued to be inexplicable – a problem with many Hamlets – that the Prince did not dispose at once of Claudius and rally loyal Denmark to his flag: no need for a Ghost's second visit to whet an almost blunted purpose. If the production was abruptly matter-of-course, and the cast – except for Rosalind Iden, Payne's daughter, and two or three others – could be the frailer trellis, Wolfit's gusto and dynamism drove on the night. One might have heard him say 'I have cause, and will, and strength and means to do 't', though as he was playing the cut version, I doubt whether one ever did. Far from the 'sweet prince', which was not in his gift, his breadth and energy had to be acknowledged: he reminded me of a Cornish local preacher at St Anthony-in-Meneage who (so my mother would tell us) added to any announcement of a hymn, 'Let there be no creepin' back, brothers! Sound him out loud and sound him out fierce!' You never knew Wolfit to be creeping back.

This was the only London *Hamlet* until an almost uncanny double event by Robert Helpmann, an Australian actor and dancer, who at thirty-three first interpreted the play at the New Theatre as a dance-drama for the Sadler's Wells company. A fluent and versatile dancer, with a developed sense of the macabre, he had always wished to act the Shakespearian Hamlet: as a prelude, he expressed it (the music used was a romantic Tchaikovsky overture) through a dream-vision, a series of images that whirled across a distorted mind as the man lay waiting to die: a surrealistic frenzy in which at one moment the Queen (Celia Franca) and Ophelia (Margot Fonteyn) were confused in psychological conflict. Leslie Hurry's setting, with its dominant avenging figure, was as disturbing as the action: Helpmann, who had asked Hurry for 'a decadent palace invested with the brooding sense of its imminent destruction', got what he required, and more. 'It will be the play next,' Horace Horsnell of the *Observer* said to us as we left the theatre in the black-out, and he was justified in 1944, twenty months later. Helpmann had done some Shakespeare for Guthrie at the Vic, where his Oberon was compared to a shimmering stag-beetle and he was anxious for this full challenge at the New in a production of *Hamlet* by Guthrie and a younger but extremely visual director, Michael Benthall. Again Leslie Hurry designed the set: certainly cluttered, but James Agate need not have been so contemptuously dismissive, 'a combination of the old Café Royal and the approach to Liverpool Street Station'. Fretful more than passionate, Helpmann was a slight, darting figure trapped in the hold of a Castle Dangerous lit only by flashes, hardly ever in the plain light of day: an inky cloak for Elsinore. Memory retains an odd sleek quality;

Helpmann's way of turning the verse into much the same lengths of shot-silk; his irony with Rosencrantz and Guildenstern; and his strained face when (the Guinness business from the Vic) he beat a tattoo on a property drum at 'The play's the thing'. Hardly the expectancy and rose of the fair state – had he reached the throne Elsinore might have been a place helpful to the arts but seldom one for the higher diplomacy: Claudius (Basil Sydney) would have been decidedly more efficient.

II

I had contributed steadily to the *Observer* since the death of the *Post*. The office, conducted with an unvaried ritual, was as hushed as a cloister; weekly, writers appeared with some ceremonial to hand in their sheaves and withdraw again into an unmapped outer world. Telephoning on a Tuesday, Harmer would tell me what to do, and on Friday I would slip into his office with the results. This could not last, yet it went on until the spring of 1942 when, soon after Garvin had broken with the Astors who owned the paper, Ivor Brown, drama critic and Shakespearian, became editor, a challenge that gratified him, even if his response was monosyllabic. Within nine or ten months I was his literary editor, used in time to the visits of such people as Harold Nicolson, infinitely urbane; George Orwell, with his own brand of sardonic gentleness, who gave an impression, entirely false, that he enjoyed nothing less than book-reviewing; and Lionel Hale, wittiest young journalist of his day, who absorbed every novel like an enquiring sponge. Often I deputised for Ivor Brown in the theatre besides going on to write for several other papers (*Punch* was one during the long absence of its critic, Eric Keown). After years of wondering what might come next, everything came at once and led, irresistibly, to the theatre.

III

Stratford kept going during war-time summers less festive than ever (the epithet had long been doubtful) but at least preserving its annual record. Internally, back-stage and front-of-house, the Memorial Theatre had grown shabbier while the streets outside were unnaturally doleful and, until a late influx of American troops, emptier. During 1942 George Hayes, at fifty-four, played a tired autumnal Hamlet, speaking with unflawed melody but as a static recital rather than a performance newly examined. That was in Ben Iden Payne's last season before he left unobtrusively for America. Honoured for his quiet personal felicities rather than for any marked theatrical force, he had not come to terms with Stratford-upon-Avon and in his autobiography he gave only a dozen lines to his eight Memorial years.

When we next met *Hamlet* there Stratford was directed by Robert Atkins, a loved and practical dictator and an actor through four decades; in youth he had been with Tree and Forbes-Robertson. His voice, like a slow rumble of incoming tide through a sea cavern, had caused him to be the most parodied man in a profession that delighted in parody: 'Do it this way, old son!' He had to cope at once with the Stratford stage which, through a quirk of planning, had always seemed curiously remote from the house. In every revival during two years he brought the action right forward so that his players had not to project themselves across a gulf. His Hamlet was John Byron, in age not yet the prescribed thirty years, in aspect a romantic with the underrated gift of charm, but in speech a man fully aware of the darker side: it was a creation apart from the festival's run-of-the-mill.

That winter of 1944 (Haymarket), John Gielgud had his fourth major Hamlet (directed by the Cambridge don,

George Rylands). Observing the corrupt Court with an even deeper bitterness, he moved still upon a flashing stream of speech. At the last, as a final loyal service, Horatio placed the crown of Denmark in his grasp. From a debut in 'the morn and liquid dew of youth' Gielgud had reconsidered his Hamlets. Today, after allowing for the 'sway of opinion', which was Garvin and Harmer's favourite headline-phrase on matters more global, I imagine the 1934 production is most regarded. Everybody, we gather, shares in Hamlet: Gielgud of 1934 is possibly the man I would have liked to be (though with several speeches from the uncanny mind of Ernest Milton quivering in the memory). From the 1944 revival I recall Peggy Ashcroft's bewildered sorrow and Cecil Trouncer as a transpontine First Player, obviously a popular star of the Danish pomping folk: he could have looked well in the voluminous fur-collared overcoat from a modern-dress revival.

Ivor Brown, who admired Gielgud profoundly and of whom I saw much, was always liable to write such things of *Hamlet* as 'It is only a failure to readers who are crazy about consistency and rake the text for trouble.' He said this to me, in effect, more than once. Not easy to know, for his reserve could breed shyness in others, he was an endeared friend and should have been an example to intractable colleagues ('The critic can be mannerly without being misleading'). To the service of the stage, and as an editor, he brought his exact mind, Balliol-trained, and his talent for swift decision. As a writer, watchfully elegant, he disliked any vagueness of word or method, loathing the officialese he called Barnacular after the Dickensian Barnacles of the Circumlocution Office. It saddened him that, through office politics, he had to leave criticism too soon: Fleet Street, in any matter that affects the arts, can be blinkered.

IV

When the war and the black-out had ended, the theatre, both metropolitan and provincial, was entering the future not as a carbon-copy of its old self, but as something fresh and contentious. Already London had had two superb classical seasons, Gielgud's at the Haymarket, and at the New the Old Vic company's which, though it reached its perihelion early (*Richard III, Uncle Vanya*) would have years ahead of it. Peace meant much also to a smaller enterprise, the Arts near Leicester Square, most distinguished club of its period and praised as 'a pocket national theatre'. An actor, Alec Clunes, had rescued and renewed it during 1942. In October 1945, at a festival of English drama, Clunes, who was six-feet-two in height, not strictly handsome but able to seem so, with a great deal of unsynthetic charm, and a baritone voice in its high summer, acted the Hamlet most people said he should have done long before. With an actor-manager's prerogative he played only what he wished: in Hamlet he recognised a personal duty. He had been Laertes to Maurice Evans at the Old Vic. Within a decade he would be Claudius in the West End. Midway, here was the man himself. In performance Clunes gained from the peculiar intimacy at so small a theatre. If opinions were even more various than usual, most agreed that it was a 'sweet prince' carried off to lie in state while Horatio – whose valediction we have to miss – was telling a yet unknowing world how these things came about.

Clunes might have been astonished to learn from one admirer that his 'Castiglionean Hamlet was more than Italian, it was European in the wider sense'. He would have preferred James Agate, who had bickered dogmatically with him at the opening of the revived Arts – Clunes could be a potent debater – and who now complimented him on his virility and tenderness; citing, moreover, 'What a piece of work is a man' and 'Nay, do not think I flatter', Agate insisted that he had 'never heard the prose in this great poem' given better; about the poetry he was less persuaded. Critics, Noël Coward had said years before, could find it hard to notice one work 'without mentioning at least sixty-five others in various stages of mental and physical decomposition'.* Not going so far, I did feel that Clunes wanted something of the larger excitement. He concentrated in detail upon one of the many Hamlets, not the darker and more passionate: everybody had to be Horatio to a boyish student of Wittenberg forced on the rack of royal Elsinore. His pulse, as ours, temperately kept time: waiting for an excitement slow to come, we reached the true presence only after the return to Denmark: the elegiac meditation among the tombs and the often scamped scene with Horatio before Osric's intrusion. It is most tempting to suppose that Hamlets were shifting in mood according to the moods of the day; but little appeared to me yet to be influenced by external events. The Arts offered honourably an actor's night in an ample text; the production by Judith Furse a lucid diagram fortified by Mark Dignam's smiling villain of a Claudius, metallic fox rather than 'bloat King'. This in any event was the festival's heart, a bonus for theatre people who, like Boswell, were naturally clubbable.

When Clunes took *Hamlet* to twenty European towns as part of a British Council repertory – 'European in the wider sense' indeed – a young Belgian chambermaid, finding no name on a laundry bundle, resourcefully copied a label on his cabin trunk: he was known thereafter as Monsieur Heavy Baggage. A cheerful tour; on his return Monsieur Heavy Baggage was saying in a book review, and neither realising nor, for that matter, caring how unfashionable this

* Coward's preface to Agate's *The Contemporary Theatre, 1924*

might sound a few years on: 'I think we should avoid the temptation to be pessimistic about our theatre – it seems to me quite one of the healthiest there is.'

7
ROUND THE CASTLES:
1945–52

I

THERE had been alarums at Stratford. For three years from the spring of 1946 Sir Barry Jackson, the Birmingham Repertory's creator, a philanthropist and civilised visionary of the theatre, had controlled the Memorial. As a governor, he had had little to do with Stratford during the dark period of the mid-thirties and later when the town, accredited shrine, was in some ways an example of the feudal-parochial. It was a distinction then to be an Old Vic Shakespearian; news that So-and-So would be appearing at Stratford impressed nobody. The Memorial needed an administrator expert in the theatre at large and able to absorb domestic problems. Robert Atkins, vigorous and tactless, speaking his mind to the right people at the wrong times, could not be the answer. At length, in an hour of resurgence, the Board turned to Barry Jackson: he was a Shakespearian, he knew all that man could know about repertory; and the near-decade in which he had ruled an annual summer month at Malvern spoke for his Festival knowledge. Now, with expansive plans that would need a few years to develop, he began to chip off the rust of complacency and false tradition: he restored the neglected theatre, chose directors of varying methods, and made Stratford attractive to London actors who had not thought twice of what some termed burial alive. In his first season he brought from Birmingham Repertory two young people who would become glittering names: the director Peter Brook and the actor Paul Scofield.

To the outer world chaos had resolved itself: certainly London papers had rediscovered Stratford. Yet by the end of 1947 Jackson and his new chairman of governors, from the town's ruling Flower family, were politely at odds, mainly because the younger man could neither appreciate a form of benign dictatorship nor realise the acute sensitivity behind it. When, in pique, Jackson resigned, the governors took too easily the cue not to renew his contract. Nevertheless, history has shown that Barry Jackson began the Stratford renaissance, a period during which what had been an ignored museum-piece rose into a power-house of the British stage.

Jackson was still in charge during April 1948 when, as usual, the world's flags fluttered through central Stratford for Shakespeare's birthday. That afternoon I noticed Paul Scofield leaning over the Tramway Bridge and staring, perhaps longingly, into the Avon: a tall, spare, high-cheekboned figure, the forehead deep-lined under dark curling hair, a face strangely Elizabethan as if it looked out from a miniature by Isaac Oliver. He was playing Hamlet at night: with this only a few hours off, any actor might have felt unnerved. As it was, the performance had no trace of strain, even if the young Elizabethan was here an early Victorian (of the year 1848) in black frock-coat and narrow strapped trousers. Michael Benthall, who directed, proclaimed that Hamlet was Everyman – no quarrel there – and that in Elizabethan costume most of his 'essential modern realism' would be lost: 'I have aimed at retaining the romance and present-day truth by presenting it in a mid-nineteenth century setting. In this way I hope to retain the magic of the theatre without destroying the play's vital contemporary relevance.'

That was a long way round. Rather than talking of contemporary relevance, it would have been better, far more candid, to say it would be fun to see how *Hamlet* might look in an Elsinore of frock-coat, crinoline and military scarlet. If there was no valid reason for the idea, at least it did not hinder: the play asserted itself immediately, and the staging became of minor account. Hamlet, never a sentimentalised abstraction, was the man most of us knew. Appalled by his father's death, his mother's too hasty marriage, the Ghost's injunction, and riven by doubt and fear – has the Ghost deceived him but to damn him? – other things heighten his despair, his loathing of 'the unweeded garden'. There is the comfort of friendship with Horatio. For the rest, the time is out of joint: 'O cursed spite, / That ever I was born to set it right.' Imaginative, lonely, needing affection, Ophelia lost ('Forty thousand brothers / Could not, with all their quantity of love, / Make up my sum'), prompted to his revenge by heaven and hell, he is bound upon a wheel of fire. Scofield was this Hamlet, romantic and haunted, 'most dreadfully attended' by the thronging phantoms of his brain. As A. V. Cookman put it in *The Times*, he 'sought not so desperately the fulfilment of his earthly mission as some steadfast refuge from the hard-driven imagination. Only in death the refuge is found.' From the first, Scofield's Hamlet was a spirit in torment no less agonising than his father's. The voice, taut or huskily caressing, had a widening range, whether in the outburst of 'O, what a rogue and peasant slave' or in the wrung heartbreak, face folded in sorrow, of 'When you are desirous to be blest, / I'll blessing beg of you'.

Pictorially, Benthall and his designer, James Bailey, had conceived a romanticised Victorian-Gothic Elsinore, a Winterhalter-Waterhouse Doubting Castle, a perspective of fretted receding arches lit by blazing chandeliers. Anthony Quayle (who soon would follow Jackson at Stratford) saw Claudius as a bluff, rubious intriguer in mutton-chop whiskers, a six-bottle man given to churchyard conspiracy with Laertes as they loitered, top-hats in hand, after Ophelia's funeral, now on a fine day. Diana Wynyard's Gertrude, red-wigged, heavy-eyed, was compared to the Empress Eugenie. Polonius (John Kidd) seemed to be a cross between a prim lawyer and a sub-standard Disraeli; and Claire Bloom's Ophelia, in her floating blue crinoline – she entered skimming like the lapwing–Beatrice★ – did not turn everything to favour and prettiness: she went wholly and vehemently mad. A good actor, Esmond Knight, was the noisiest Ghost I have heard: possibly a change to have so passionate a spectre, vociferous and asthmatic, but there was something too solid for the majesty of buried Denmark. Shaw might have said of him, as he did once of Ian Robertson: 'The voice is not a bad voice, but it is the voice of a man who does not believe in ghosts. Moreover, it is a hungry voice, not that of one who is past eating.' When Esmond Knight appeared in the Queen's closet we observed that, being a good Victorian, he had punctiliously exchanged his uniform for a dressing-gown.

Robert Helpmann, Hamlet at alternate performances, was reasoned, supple, and technically exact, but without Scofield's special illumination. The director's use of naked candlelight, which glimmered eerily in the cavern of the Stratford stage, took me to an obvious analogy: while Helpmann was like an electric candle, clear and formal, Scofield's flame could waver across every corner of shadowed Elsinore. This year the Festival company had a private joke, the supposed alarm of Queen Victoria and the Prince Consort on receiving orders to murder Rosencrantz and Guildenstern. Tactfully, Benthall omitted the English

★ 'For look where Beatrice, like a lapwing, runs / Close by the ground to hear our conference'. *Much Ado About Nothing*, III.1

ambassadors from the last scene. Maybe they had no vital contemporary relevance.

II

Almost at once we moved from theatre to cinema. The only *Hamlet* film I had known was a late showing of a silent classic made as far back as 1913 and from which I remember only Forbes-Robertson hastening along a beach (it was Lulworth Cove), and an early scene in which the Marcellus was Robert Atkins, identifiable at once by the four-square stance so familiar down the years. Filmed Shakespeare had usually evaded me, though I had a diary note about an *As You Like It* in 1936: 'Elisabeth Bergner as the archest, most infuriating kind of Rosalind-Pan. A flock of sheep. Another flock of sheep. A sugary, tea-gardenish, Epping-on-Bank-Holiday setting; an over-populated forest. Laurence Olivier's Orlando stopped at every turn by his coy and romping Rosalind.' During the war there had been Olivier's own grandly conceived *Henry V*, beginning in the deliberate artifice of its Globe Theatre scenes and expanding into a grand Shakespearian surge.

Now, in 1948, we had Olivier's *Hamlet*, not in colour but in black-and-white, from an enclosed world massively claustrophobic and prefaced (by Olivier himself) with the arguable simplification, 'This is the tragedy of a man who could not make up his mind.' Black-and-white was used, rather than colour, 'to achieve through depth of focus a more majestic, more poetic image, in keeping with the stature of the verse'. I went to a preview expecting, rashly, to recapture a memory, to hear this Hamlet thrusting again through scenes prized still from goodness knows how many Old Vic nights and from the Danish ground itself. But here, on the screen, was a new earth – certainly a new Elsinore – and a less apparent heaven. Nothing could entirely replace for me the fervour of eleven years before. Olivier had decided to change the colour of his hair to Scandinavian blond, reasonable enough as a means of making Hamlet more conspicuous, as he should be, in middle and long shots, yet I had a nagging sense that this could falsify the man, alter the complexion of his mind. He looked now and again like a version – agreed, far handsomer – of the stiff engravings in the mid-Victorian Cowden Clarke edition, or maybe like the actor Charles Fechter.

I worried less about the transformation of the castle into a place of interminable corridors, coiled staircases, caverns measureless to man, though I should have done so because clearly it was an idol to which much of the verse had been sacrificed. But it could be said that Roger Furse's towering Elsinore, with its torch-bright council chamber, was more dramatically Hamlet's castle than Helsingör's Kronborg by the flat Danish coast. Anyway, Shakespeare's Elsinore is not that of Denmark any more than it is the poet Campbell's when he invokes 'thy wild and stormy steep'. Its heights, in the film, returned me to those first readings at the Lizard when the Rill Head was the 'dread summit of the cliff / That beetles o'er his base into the sea'. What I missed during the restless wandering up and down was the concentrated urgency, the strung-wire tension of 1937.

Olivier said, though he grew to dislike the phrase, that his work should be regarded as 'an essay in *Hamlet*'. It had had to be abridged, only two and a half hours of it, and in the shredding and patching much had to go. What seemed quite unnecessary was the resolve by Olivier and his text editor, Alan Dent, critic, Shakespeare specialist and disarming Scot, that various lines should be clarified, as if listeners would withdraw their attention in the middle of a speech to ask what this-or-the-other meant. The alterations may not have been numerous; they were superfluities, that could fidget one like comparably useless changes in the newest revision of the Bible. Thus, 'like the King that's dead' became 'like the dead king Hamlet'. Claudius urged Hamlet not to 'persist' (instead of 'persever') in obstinate condolement. We had 'roar' for 'bruit' in the line of the 'King's rouse'; 'suffer' instead of 'beteem,' and 'minds not his own creed' for 'recks not his own rede'. 'I'll make a ghost of him that *hinders* me,' cried Hamlet, instead of 'lets me'. The superb 'That would be scanned', as Hamlet waited behind the King kneeling at prayer, was altered to 'That would be thought on'; and – if I recall – his father was not allowed Hyperion's curls. I could not agree that 'thus hath hoodwinked you' was a happy substitute for 'thus hath cozened you at hoodman-blind', or that 'your true lord' had the ring of 'your precedent lord'. And so forth. We had to read 'madness' for 'ecstasy'. The hectic in the blood was thinned to the fever in the blood. The 'general gender' became 'the general people'; we had 'venomed *point*' for 'stuck', and towards the end 'sticks fiery off indeed' turned to 'shines indeed'.

It was dangerous, as always, to blur the Shakespearian sound. Further to trim the film to a workable length, and to allow for time spent on stair-and-corridor work – not that we could mourn 'sapless perambulation', an Oxford verdict on another *Hamlet* long before – there had been a number of sad cuts. Rosencrantz and Guildenstern 'went to't' in the most downright sense; they were removed bodily. So was Fortinbras. So, most seriously, recalling its extraordinary power at the Vic, was that test for any Hamlet, 'How all occasions do inform against me!', a twelfth-hour cut that Olivier regretted: 'From a film-maker's point of view it was not a time to get discursive, and so I cut it for purely filmic reasons.' Transpositions as well. I thought for a while, incredulous, that Hamlet would lose the homage to Horatio. No; it arrived near the end, sandwiched between the Osric and duel scenes, and it was there that Olivier, back to his old quality, reached the heart. I think also of the gentleness of 'Rest, rest, perturbèd spirit'; the speaking of 'To be or not to be', meditation on suicide, while Hamlet looked down, many fathoms, from a high tower and heard the sea roaring beneath; the advice to the Players; and the wry tenderness of 'Make him laugh at that' in the Yorick scene. The duel was intricately protracted; and the 1937 Olivier was there in the swift leap upon the King. Four captains bore the dead Hamlet through the castle to the topmost tower, a superb processional end to a play that faded in majesty; nothing became it like its close.

Yet, all considered, the film *Hamlet*, with its Prince blondly incongruous in that raven-haired assembly, lacked the steady thrill of other days and circumstances. In spite of moments of needled perception and a few scenes that did snatch us from the cinema to the zenith of Shakespearian playing, Olivier rarely struck us to the soul: he was an older Hamlet, not a better. Some pictures stayed with me: Elsinore by night in a glistening sea-mist, the ultimate mêlée of the Play scene. A man-about-the-cinema, his Shakespeare on the shelf, might find it less dashing than *Henry V*, but he would appreciate technique and controlled opulence, and if the film beckoned him to the play proper, it would have done some service. I liked Basil Sydney's Claudius, reminiscent of Holbein's Henry VIII; Anthony Quayle's Marcellus – no fear of that actor, a seasoned man-round-Elsinore, throwing away 'the bird of dawning'; and the perpetually watchful Horatio of Norman Wooland. Jean Simmons, at seventeen, was a very simple Ophelia, her death shown (as it might have been in the Millais picture) while the Queen was describing it, not a very fruitful idea. Eileen Herlie was an undistinguished Gertrude until (we were surprised to observe) her suicide, knowingly taking the poisoned cup and smiling in death. Collectors noted that the Ghost was an eerie fuzz from which Olivier's voice emerged; that Francisco (seven lines) was John

Laurie, himself a former Old Vic Hamlet; that Hamlet's first lines were, unexpectedly, 'Ay, madam, it is common'; and that, briefly, we had a flash of the Prince adventuring, in mime, on the high seas, to illustrate the letter to Horatio: 'Ere we were two days old at sea, a pirate of very warlike appointment gave us chase.'

Achievement though it was, the film could have been less teasingly planned. Jock Dent, always calm when assailed, said amiably, his erudition wasted, I fear, that at least he had done nothing to the text like Schiller's effort, in a German *Macbeth*, to regularise the Bleeding Sergeant speech.

III

There had been the kind of reconstruction at the *Observer* that, in the too predictable rhythms of newspaper life, any fresh editor feels obliged to make, especially one wholly different in method from Ivor Brown and without his dedication to the arts. Though I would remain with Brown for his last Tudor Street years, I worked now, having become a pluralist in criticism, from our house in Hampstead: there, through the next four decades, half a lifetime, I would be given entirely to the theatre and its history, present and past.

In several seasons, from the summer of 1948, the two most valuable *Hamlets*, one far more publicised than the other, were directed by Hugh Hunt, who had worked with a personal blend of scholarship and theatrical zest in the green-and-gold casket of the restored Bristol Old Vic. The London stage for a quartet of repertory plays from various parts of England was the St James's, a historic house (its sight-lines, alas, were equally historic), replaced later by a sullen office block. In the Bristol *Hamlet* Robert Eddison, at forty, impetuous, febrile, deep in grief, with what were called 'the eyes of a hunted fawn', spoke with a nervous beauty. Always princely, Eddison, as through his career, could dignify a room by entering it.

In Hunt's second production, during 1950, he had left Bristol for the London Old Vic in its final months at the New (today's Albery): we could contemplate the company's return, after ten years, to the theatre of 'acanthus leaves, Prince of Wales's feathers, and gas-bracket rococo' and that 'neat frieze of plaster lace painted with gilded custard'. (This description is by Alan Pryce-Jones, later editor of the *Times Literary Supplement*.) The company had begun in so high a temperature at the New that nobody was really startled when the thermometer had to drop. Hunt, a director with a talent for unifying his company, could prevent the farewell to the West End from being in any way an anti-climax. He had begun with *Love's Labour's Lost*, comedy of courtly revel and the gleam of Shakespeare's April – irritated, a German sage dismissed it as 'excessively jocular' – that fades into twilight and dew-fall, and at the last into country song. Good; but I had waited for *Hamlet*, certain that it would share at least one quality with Ben Greet's swiftly assembled production at the Plymouth Theatre Royal a quarter of a century earlier. Neither director, old or new, had approached the play as a crux to be pondered interminably (Greet would have asked why, his voice sharply frosted), and neither chose to present it in the modes of William-and-Mary in the thickest murk upon a polygon. They knew the simple truth that text-manipulators forget; left alone, it can speak for itself with most miraculous organ. Though people will analyse it while time endures, some of us wince from such a phrase as this in a published study: 'It is as though Shakespeare's own axes of reference in the imaginative world are sus-pect.' The critic Lionel Hale murmured: 'Lucky he didn't know that!'

Michael Redgrave, just before his forty-second birthday, was an actor of heroic aspect who appeared to have every gift, mental and physical. What this Hamlet needed was the final stir and sting of excitement, the ultimate levin-flash, something that can be denied to an actor otherwise technically irreproachable. (Ernest Milton had it through life, even when his mannerisms had proliferated: 'Any fool can pick on mannerisms' the *Guardian* critic, Philip Hope-Wallace, said curtly.) Redgrave, as we had known he would, moved with unmannered ease and what T. C. Worsley, of the *New Statesman*, would call 'an absolute mastery of the vocal line', especially in the soliloquies. His Hamlet, shaken to the depths, would never lose our respect though, when the night was over, some were asking whether respect could not have been mingled with un-complicated theatrical excitement.

The production began unsurely, tameness on the 'platform' and at first in the Court; it took Hunt a little time to find a key to Elsinore. From the Nunnery scene onwards Redgrave took charge intellectually, not just as a pedant's prowling question mark. (He rejected the Oedipus complex.) We marked such things as the curl of the lip when Hamlet, aware of deceit, saw Ophelia's prayer-book ('Nymph, in thy orisons . . .'); the advice to the Players, treated very simply, with no overplus of condescension; at the end of 'The play's the thing' the lifting of a crown above his head from the visitors' property-basket; the swirling of a great red cloak; the dangerous glint of the 'recorders' speech to Guildenstern; the Closet scene when, at 'the counterfeit presentment of two brothers,' he employed the locket that he wore, bearing a miniature of his father, and a coin with Claudius's head; and the cogency of 'How all occasions', a soliloquy that, more than any, can speak for the man: it was always a disaster to cut this from the short version. There was, above all, the passage before the duel when Hamlet, who had occasionally been too detached, seized us in the lines to Horatio, 'Not a whit, we defy augury,' and what followed. From the entire night the two words, 'Let be', stay clearly over the gulf of years: Hunt might almost have used them as an epigraph. It could have been argued, I suppose, that Rosencrantz and Guildenstern, exercises in the slithy tove, were perilous, but I had cherished the idea of them, seldom established in perform-ance, as raffish-sinister hangers-on, no credit to Witten-berg, who must excite our loathing. Was I thinking for myself in feeling no pang – Hamlet, 'sweet prince', did not – that this pair must meet instant doom at the English Court? Hamlet would have trusted them as he would a pair of adders:

> Why, man, they did make love to this employment;
> They are not near my conscience; their defeat
> Does by their own insinuation grow;
> 'Tis dangerous when the baser nature comes
> Between the pass and fell incensed points
> Of mighty opposites.

Scribbled notes bring back small things elsewhere. I was conscious, for the first time, of Laertes crying to somebody unseen, 'My necessaries are embark'd, farewell', before turning to Ophelia, one of those moments when, as Professor Arthur Colby Sprague has said in an entertaining essay, a character enters direct from a conversation. A word, 'Precepts', reminds me that towards the end of the Polonius speech his children silently mouthed, 'To thine own self be true . . .', an injunction that would have bored them since childhood. Claudius, rushing from the throne after 'The Mouse-trap', aimed a blow at the First Player. Ophelia, in distraction, thrust the 'rue', a wisp of straw, in the Queen's hair at the line, 'You must wear your rue with a difference.' The First Gravedigger (George Benson) illust-rated the old jest about the man who goes to the water and the water that comes to the man by propping his own hat upon the skull of Yorick. Redgrave, in the rant, preferred 'Woo't drink up *Nilus*? eat a crocodile?' to the more familiar 'eisel' (vinegar). Claudius, defeated, lifted his crown as if divine right might save him; and Hamlet, near death, held momentarily the crown he had snatched from the dying King.

Much of the playing that night was helpful: Mark Dignam's steel-trap Claudius and a carefully-weighted, sensual Queen (Wanda Rotha) – their passion we could credit; it had not always been so – Walter Hudd's Polonius, a tremulous silver fox, and the Ophelia (Yvonne Mitchell), refusing to be conscious of a show-part that is often sister to Sheridan's Tilburina, mad in white satin.

IV

Round these Hamlets there were three or four that, by comparison, I can summon only patchily. Donald Wolfit, while searching for a London home, had some months (1949) in the ornate surroundings of the Bedford Theatre where Sickert had painted its ornate gilt in the dead vast and middle of Camden High Street. Bravely accepting that he had outgrown Hamlet (he was forty-six) he resigned the part to Joseph O'Conor, aged thirty-three, then and thereafter an unfailing Shakespearian: his performance, ruler-straight without a touch of neurosis, was likeable for its modesty and its resolve to let no particle of drama elude him. Wolfit, having exchanged the apron of First Grave-digger – and he was the earthiest of functionaries – for formal evening dress, led Hamlet on paternally at the end.

At Guildford Repertory in 1951 – the present Yvonne Arnaud Theatre was then far ahead – Laurence Payne, who had been a Stratford Romeo, spoke with brisk certainty in a design for a more detailed portrait; some of this was visible at the Embassy, Hampstead, during 1953. At Guildford he was matched by Robert Marsden, expressing the attributes of a Claudius who, for all his draughts of Rhenish, was a regal statesman. That year, when John Harrison directed at the tiny New Boltons in Kensington, David Markham might not have had a classical-romantic actor's full equipment – vocally there was a scratch of the thistle – but he did suggest, as relatively few Hamlets do, a life before the play: he had not just moved on from the wings. Sometimes the intimacy of a very small theatre seems to quicken the imagination of both actor and audience as it did then.

David Williams, in an Oxford University Dramatic Society production (1952), used a sound plain text version that he and Nevill Coghill had trimmed discreetly. Though his performance, cool, aloof, alertly poised and phrased, held the sharp line of a glass-cutter's diamond, we had to ask if this Hamlet had ever had bad dreams. I think, too, from what I have to call By-Path Meadow, of a 1948 production by Oxford undergraduates at a hall in the backlands of Baker Street. This employed costumes and décor of 'a sophisticated European Court in the third quarter of the eighteenth century; the emphasis is on quizzing-glasses, port, and politesse'. Unfortunately, and without a quizzing-glass, my attention must have strayed: wrongly, because the night's text, meant for collectors, was the pirated First Quarto of 1603, resting upon the memory of a forgotten Marcellus. High-spirited extravagance is the sole impression that remains.

8
IN FESTIVAL: 1951–56

I

AFTER the quick, quiet, delicate Ruritanian Hamlet of Alec Guinness when he was in league with Guthrie at the Old Vic during 1938, we had hoped for high revelation in 1951. It was then, Festival of Britain year, that he directed himself, with the help of Frank Hauser of the BBC, at the New Theatre, so often a window of the classical stage. The summer's rush was inimical to second visits. I regretted seeing Guinness only once, on the night of May 17, an occasion fated from the start. He had rebelled, so we understood, against the Shakespeare style to which he had been bred: he saw 'no reason for making God's gift to the actor – a flat, square stage – into something like the entrance to the Athenaeum.' Hopeful though it sounded, not much lingers from a night stripped of theatrical ivy. (We can ignore transient lighting confusion, a switchboard muddle that would not recur.) The set was perfectly simple. No rostra ('Apart from cluttering the stage, they tend to produce a one-foot-up, one-foot-down sort of act which I find peculiarly dispiriting'). Hamlet did not see the King and Polonius on watch during the Nunnery scene. The King and Queen let the dumbshow pass without alarm. The First Player did not speak the poisoner's lines. Hamlet did not make off with the King's sword after 'Now might I do it pat.' On with the play: no

call to bother about inventive commentators or earlier
directors. Still, the world's most exciting play – the
adjective is bound to return – failed to excite. Directness,
lucidity, yes (though it would have been wise to cut the
searchlight on the King's face in the Play scene, and the
Player King's phosphorescent crown). I felt at the première
that nobody, or hardly anybody, in the cast was in tune
with *Hamlet*: the unluckiest moment came when an
impeccably modern Laertes, on being told that his sister
was drowned, remarked 'O, where?' as if he were responding to casual gossip of the district. Guinness himself, a
slight figure with moustache and goatee beard that aged
him, and heavy with many cares, looked as if he would
track down Hamlet, given the chance, and undoubtedly
several speeches, 'O, what a rogue and peasant slave' for
one, showed what could have happened at a more
propitious hour. We knew he was a magnificent actor. The
house, gallery excepted, seemed to be alive with sympathy;
but it was not his night: possibly no man, even with help in
the production, should have taken on so much. Kenneth
Tynan, the night's First Player, temporarily an actor before
moving to drama criticism, wrote sadly: 'Having cut
himself adrift from safe Shakespeare tradition, he resigned
the tiller and left the production becalmed. It was *Hamlet*
with the pilot dropped.'

II

Now, for two years, nothing: that is, plenty of Shakespeare, but the roads to Elsinore closed. During the
summer of 1951 we went back to The Lizard. There my
oldest neighbour, getting on for ninety and seeking to cheer
me in what was plainly a baffling life, said that her son had
gone to London, for her a meaningless name. She added
soothingly: 'Well, you'll be seeing him, I shouldn't

John Barrymore as
Hamlet with the Queen,
his mother (Constance
Collier), in the Closet
scene: Haymarket,
1925.

Barrymore watches the
King (Malcolm Keen) at
prayer. 'Now might I
do it pat.'

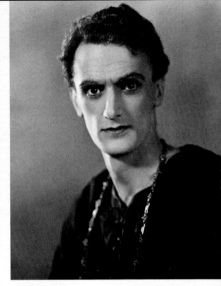

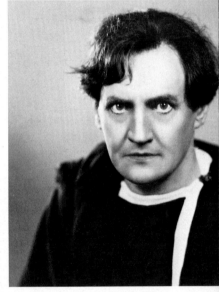

ABOVE LEFT: Ernest Milton played Hamlet for the Old Vic in 1919 and on many later occasions; the last (as in this photograph) was in April 1925.
ABOVE RIGHT: John Laurie, when 32, at the Old Vic in April 1929. The following year he was Claudius at the Royal Court.
ABOVE: Henry Ainley played Hamlet at the Haymarket in April 1930, when he was fifty.

Maurice Evans (Old Vic, 1935) as Hamlet – in a production by Henry Cass – which he played in both the 'eternity' and the short versions during his last season before leaving for the United States.

TOP: Robert Harris in the Graveyard scene, Old Vic, April 1932, with Ralph Richardson (*right*) as First Gravedigger.

ABOVE LEFT: John Gielgud dies in the arms of Horatio (Jack Hawkins), New Theatre, November 1934. 'Now cracks a noble heart. Good night, sweet prince.'

ABOVE RIGHT: Alec Guinness, with the skull of Yorick – 'I knew him, Horatio: a fellow of infinite jest, of most excellent fancy' – in Tyrone Guthrie's modern-dress production of *Hamlet*, acted in its entirety at the Old Vic during the autumn of 1938.

LEFT: Donald Wolfit appeared first as Hamlet at Stratford-upon-Avon in 1936 and later at many times and places.
RIGHT: John Neville with Judi Dench as Ophelia ('My lord I have remembrances of yours/That I have longed long to re-deliver'): Old Vic, 1957.

FAR RIGHT: Michael Redgrave wit[h] Dorothy Tutin (Ophelia) in the Stratford-upon-Avon *Hamlet,* 195[8] 'Get thee to a nunnery. Why woul[d] thou be a breeder of sinners?'
BELOW: The final scene in Glen By[am] Shaw's production at Stratford-up[on] Avon, 1958. The duellists are Mic[hael] Redgrave (*right*) and Edward Woodward (*left*). Behind them, on[e] of the steps, are Mark Dignam (Claudius) and Googie Withers (Gertrude).

Alec Clunes at the Arts Theatre, London, in October 1945.

LEFT: Robert Helpmann, Australian-born dancer and actor, appeared during 1942 in a *Hamlet* ballet at what was then the New Theatre, and in 1944 (also at the New) in Shakespeare's tragedy for the Old Vic company.

Laurence Olivier, his hair a Nordic blond, with Jean Simmons as Ophelia, in the film version, 1947.

Innokenti Smoktunovski as the Prince in Grigori Kozintsev's 1964 film version, made to mark the quatercentenary of Shakespeare's birth.

TOP: Nicol Williamson (*right*) in the duel scene at the Round House, London, March 1969.

David Warner ('O shame! where is thy blush?') reproaching Elizabeth Spriggs as the Queen ('O Hamlet, speak no more!') during the Closet scene in Peter Hall's production at Stratford-upon-Avon, 1965.

RIGHT: Derek Jacobi behind the King (Timothy West) in the Prayer scene, Old Vic, 1979.

LEFT: Roger Rees at Stratford-upon-Avon, September 1984. 'Angels and ministers of grace defend us!'

Richard Chamberlain in the production by Peter Dews at Birmingham Repertory Theatre, 1969.

Jonathan Pryce with Gertrude (Jill Bennett), Royal Court, 1980: 'Once more, good night;/And when you are desirous to be blest, I'll blessing beg of you.'

wonder, when you go down street.' (I never did.) During
this holiday I felt I had to travel to Stratford, by a quirk of
fashion and much improved internally, the most debated of
English theatres, to see the young Welsh actor, Richard
Burton, as Henry V. It was a journey of about eight hours
and it might have been better to stay in our remoteness. The
Henry, dark, stocky, and oddly inexpressive, was a
cautious sketch in monochrome.

Two years later, and before beginning an engagement at
the Old Vic, the same young man was at the Edinburgh
Festival which through seven years had played itself into
the calendar with a production of some sort in any fairly
central building capable of holding a stage. Outside,
whatever the weather, and Edinburgh would be lucky,
there was a Pentecostal confusion of accents in Princes
Street and a ceaseless hurrying of feet among the towering
'lands' of the Royal Mile. I stayed, with Eric Keown and
Ronald Searle of *Punch*, more than twenty miles away in the
castled village of Dirleton near North Berwick, and with
Berwick Law strong against the sky. An afternoon drive
into Edinburgh became annual tradition; by major golf
courses and a major battlefield (Prestonpans), across the
East Lothian levels until a grey bulk in the distance opened
into the city: a vision of crag and spire, tower and turret, the
serrated silhouette of the Old Town's ridged backbone, and
the Castle Rock that at night, floodlit, would rise like a
sustained shout.

The core of the Festival then, as it is now, was the
Assembly Hall of the Church of Scotland, entered from
steps overpeered by John Knox's statue. Tyrone Guthrie
had discovered it for a theatre in 1948 when he directed a
sixteenth-century morality, *The Thrie Estaites* (permission
freely granted so long as he did not want to do anything to
the Moderator's throne, to knock nails into it perhaps). It
was here that in 1953 Richard Burton played Hamlet – 'a

heck of a part, tosh!' he told an interviewer, something particularly important because soon it was to open Michael Benthall's five-year plan of every Shakespeare play at the Old Vic. (In the end they left out *Pericles*, for which I was wistful, remembering 'Celestial Dian, goddess argentine!') The Vic, we heard, would have a permanent set of three Palladian arches: it endured for a single season.

In Edinburgh the vast platform stage of the Assembly Hall was no director's dream, but he could bring the action into the auditorium itself and now and again I caught myself thinking of the Ghost's 'Swift as quicksilver it courses through the natural gates and alleys of the body.' Benthall encouraged his players to enter, as it were, by every gate and alley. If not noticeably like quicksilver, they worked hard. By the end of a row Ophelia would dart out in her madness, or Osric brush past, or you would turn round to find their Majesties of Denmark in procession behind the bier. There could be moments of danger. Eric Keown, beside me, all but impaled on a sword, observed with his usual philosophy, 'All right; I can begin my notice by saying, "Last night I sat transfixed".' Through the evening this swooping in the aisles grew a little tiresome: so, also, 'masking' on the platform edge. In such a complex production as Benthall's it was as inevitable as annoying to have to strain between shoulders and reflect that even if the courtiers of Denmark were a fine body of men, one back had a trick of resembling another. On occasion all was right: when Hamlet came forward to the out-thrust prow; when, at the end, he and Laertes were duelling across the great platform, and even up the steps at the back; and, much earlier, when at 'Hamlet, this deed for thine especial safety' – the last four words used to be common on safety curtains when there were any – the King, his black-cloaked courtiers round him, moved towards Hamlet, slowly and menacingly, along the platform length. Denmark was a prison.

Though Benthall craftily adjusted details to the Old Vic on a confined stage of triple arches, the essentials of the playing did not change: it was a pity because Burton was not yet a Hamlet, simply an agreeable young man without the grace, the singular charm that he should have had as the state's expectancy and rose. He lacked a communicable sense of poetry: the words were noble, their delivery painstaking and often unvaried. In the quieter passages some of Hamlet emerged, but it would not have been unfair to say that, vocally, this could be a rendering on two notes, one soft, the other loud.

He did carry the Ghost scene. On the midnight battle-ments the air bit shrewdly: Hamlet, in strung appre-hension, was talking for talking's sake. At the Ghost's appearance he would not turn: he realised that he felt the presence, that Horatio's 'Look, my lord, it comes!' was needless. Staring before him, he crossed himself: 'Angels and ministers of grace, defend us!' Could it be a spirit of health or goblin damned? He must be sure, and he questioned it (Burton missed the tenderness in the desperate 'Father!'). Steadfastly, he would not stir for what seemed to be an aeon. Then at last, as the Ghost moved, beckoning him away, Hamlet, very deliberately, did turn. A wild burst of recognition; silence. Holding his sword hilt as a cross before him, he followed slowly: his fate cried out.

That scene was theatrically potent, even if we could not believe that Hamlet would have held himself aloof so long. What succeeded it, the Ghost urging him to revenge, wavered at the première because the Ghost was solidly flesh-and-blood, and when he spoke did so in a harsh, panting wheeze, like a bronchial steam-jet. True, spectres seldom orate: this one had been silent for 'twice two months'. In the event, he could have been in the final throes of asthma, and such a pronunciation as 'My smooth bo-o-dy' scarcely made him more spectral. We agreed, on the road back, that we could have produced a better ghost, at any time, from the ruins of Dirleton Castle which pre-dated *Hamlet*.

Among the living, Fay Compton as the Queen, weary and pallid, established the conscience-frayed woman without a dubious inflection or a meaningless gesture: I would recreate her voice in the simplest lines, 'I thought thy bride-bed to have strewed, sweet maid, / And not have strewed thy grave.' William Squire, the Horatio, did not minimise one of the most constant friends in Shakespeare. Michael Hordern was a twittering, throw-away Polonius, ready for a retirement pension (a good cruel device to let him overhear Hamlet's 'These tedious old fools!'); Claire Bloom's Ophelia was a technical matter, calculated rather than affecting; and Laurence Hardy's Claudius – the poisoner Lucianus was made up to look like him – resembled a brigand crossed with a topping monk, a Friar Tuck who, to his surprise, had sailed under the Jolly Roger. Hamlet himself? Seek as I would, I could find little to add. A note, possibly, on an expressive facial flash at 'A' poisons him in th'garden for 's estate'; regret at the lapse on 'I do not know why yet I live to say / This thing's to do', among the very few Hamlets I can recall who flattened that soliloquy when they had the luck to speak it.

The night would bequeath a few felicities, such as the lantern-illuminated group in the Play scene, the King's reading of the truth in Hamlet's eyes, and the amplitude of a text (three and three-quarter hours) that enabled Hamlet, in the Closet scene, to get a second wind at 'One word more, good lady.' But I cannot say that Burton, at twenty-nine, began to sound the most daunting part in the theatre from his lowest note to the top of his compass.

III

During 1955 I was occupied in detail with a life of the

nineteenth-century tragedian, William Charles Macready, a man generally misunderstood in modern criticism. A great actor, for it would be wrong not to say so, and I am fairly sure he would have agreed, he would pity himself for belonging to an inferior calling as it was then regarded, and yet rage at any presumed insult to it. We have heard far more of his flurries of self-pity than of his loyal anger. If he brooded on degree, priority, and place, we have to recognise that he was brought up, an educated, touchy youth, in a society elaborately graded: an actor, a word to be uttered in italics, was usually an odd man out, lost in the huddle of the pomping folk on their seedy provincial pilgrimages. Macready knew his contradictions. His self-portrait, tortured and unfalteringly honest, is in the pages of his journal: there is no personal document of the stage to match it. Michéal MacLiammóir described him as 'an unwavering slow thunderbolt of a man, never asking for our sympathy, never demanding our love, always, in some Sphinx-like fashion of his own, deeply and inexplicably moving.'

Hamlet was naturally one of his favourite parts. Having often to appear in it as a visiting star with the stock companies of the day, his journal repeatedly charts his gloom: Birmingham, 1845, 'I went to the theatre, but neither actors nor manager were there, nor were they coming, it was only *Hamlet*, and they knew it quite well!!! I wish they did'; Plymouth Theatre Royal, 1846, 'The rehearsal was one of the most hopeless productions I have almost *ever* seen. Rested and thought on Hamlet, resolving not to let the inaccuracy and incompetency of these wretches! – they are no better – disturb me.'

Whatever Macready would have thought of a modern stage bewildering to him, he might have written a good deal (with some reluctant respect) of Peter Brook's development as a director. At twenty Brook had impressed

Barry Jackson, who called him 'the youngest earthquake I know', by his adventurous revivals of Shaw, Shakespeare, and Ibsen at Birmingham Repertory; he went on (after further growing pains at Stratford and opera production at Covent Garden) to use the creative gift that put him among the most logically imaginative theatre-men of his time. During the summer of 1955 he (as director) and Laurence Olivier (as actor) restored to Stratford the only play still unknown at the Memorial Theatre, a production of *Titus Andronicus*, something Macready would never have begun to ponder. Stratford, after nearly eight decades, had still kept off the agonies of the neo-Senecan drama, the raping and mutilation of Lavinia. Titus's chopping off his own hand and the final choreography of death. But on a hot August evening when the bloodstained thumb at last left its print upon the page, the audience responded to Brook's hair-spring theatre sense, his establishment (those immoderate atrocities slightly out of focus) of Rome as a remote, eerie, almost lunar world. Within it Olivier's terrifying quietness was the quiet at the core of a hurricane. In his anger he felt the storm-wind of the equinox.

That autumn *Hamlet*, for Brook in London, was an even sterner challenge. After all, few critics had known what they needed from *Titus*, though they were ready to concede that Brook had given it to them. But most people knew more or less precisely what to expect from *Hamlet*, and all were exigent. (Observing the cairn of literature about the play, Shakespeare might have quoted under his breath, 'Now pile your dust upon the quick and dead.') I saw Brook's production twice within a month, at Birmingham (where I went often then) and soon afterwards in London, at the Phoenix. Between these visits the company had gone to the Moscow Art Theatre: twenty curtain calls for the first British actors there since the 1917 Revolution.

Paul Scofield was older by seven years since his alternation with Helpmann at Stratford; his Hamlet had not changed radically except for an intensified sadness. Brook directed in a chameleon-set by Georges Wakhevitch, an arched hall, its windows, crannies, galleries, put to resourceful use: to the basic frame were added cannon, crimson hangings and the piles of a pier. Hamlet was not 'discovered' as a routine gloomy Dane, brooding and apart in the room of state. When the battlements had vanished, and lights rose upon the hall and its receding arches, there, before the Court appeared, Hamlet stood alone, gazing sadly round him until he went to his place: tall, frail (he had 'a curious moth-like fragility' said Hope-Wallace), the weary prince, not for a moment sentimentalised, who must be a soul in travail, no professors' enigma but a gentle son who loves deeply, his emotion never fabricated, one whom death and disloyalty have touched to the quick. During the progress through Hamlet's mind we marked the infinite longing in his cry of 'Father'; the anguished 'O cursed spite', Scofield's arms flung wide, all grief in that husky, rifted voice; the early tenderness for Ophelia, drawn closely to him while he spoke; at 'The play's the thing' a momentary pause, framed in a doorway, his hair tossed, eyes smouldering; the loving urgency of the homage to Horatio while sitting on the Players' property skip. Then the reversion, so it appeared, to an earlier Hamlet manner, at the vocal swell of ' 'Tis now the very witching time of night'; a passage during the Closet scene when, boy again, his head drooped upon the Queen's shoulder ('When you are desirous to be blest, I'll blessing beg of you'); the Graveyard philosophy and the Graveyard brag; the acceptance before the duel ('If it be not now, yet it will come'), a man rapt as he approached his resolution; and the royalty in his voice when in death he left name and story to the keeping of his friend.

There were doubts: this or the other shade of emotion

might have been expressed more exactly, or that scene more firmly planned; and probably – the phrase here is Agate's, but pre-Scofield – we knew that his Hamlet's mind lacked its rotting boards. He was, I felt, most poignant, anger flickering to stillness, at the simple 'I do repent' above the body of Polonius. Always we must find debate about his treatment of the verse which he could turn to desperate music; he has never been a marmoreal reciter. The test of any Hamlet is what remains with us long afterwards when there has been time for reckoning and retrospect. Some immediate critics at the Phoenix found Scofield too restrained: Anthony Hartley (the *Spectator*) held that 'the demonic, brutal character of the Renaissance prince was much underplayed, and we were left with Renaissance melancholy, the muted note of a sonnet by Du Bellay or a lyric by Nashe.' Others mourned for the younger Stratford Scofield, just as once they had missed the Gielgud of the Vic. Any Hamlet is bound to face a house divided. 'What man is living', exclaimed the rapturous Mrs Curdle (*Nicholas Nickleby*), 'who can present before us all those changing and prismatic colours with which the character is invested?' After thirty years I have not met a performance less externalised than Scofield's, able to communicate suffering without emotional pitch-and-toss; he had that within which passeth show. Brook (recalling an intense artistic fellowship) would write, in *The Empty Space*, of Scofield's acting, 'Its absolutely personal structure of rhythms, its own instinctive meanings: to rehearse a part he lets his whole nature – a milliard of super-sensitive scanners – pass to and fro across the words. In performance the same process makes everything that he has apparently fixed come back again each night the same and absolutely different.'

The company round Scofield kept to Brook's conception: Diana Wynyard as the Queen, Mary Ure as a sex-ridden Ophelia, hardly a wan pre-Raphaelite maiden,

Ernest Thesiger as a dry stick of a Polonius, unclowned, and Alec Clunes as an almost too formidably attractive Claudius who must be the satyr to the dead King's Hyperion. He liked the part because so few actors had gone down in history as the smiling, damned villain: rejecting melodrama, Clunes used the depths of his majestic baritone for a man it could be oddly impossible to condemn.

IV

A problem with recreating many players in the same part is that memories can overlap each other in shifting patterns across a long period; I have tried to keep to impressions that my notes confirm. On the Stratford *Hamlet* of 1956 they are perfectly clear. This had to be a taxing season, following as it did Olivier's with *Macbeth* and *Titus*; and Glen Byam Shaw, now full administrator (he had been sharing with Anthony Quayle) could let nothing slide. Once an actor in Gielgud's company, as a director he had much of the clarity Stratford remembered from Bridges-Adams. For actors the engagement had ceased for a decade to be an exile as hopeless as Ovid's at Tomi. The Memorial had grown into its site, looking from the opposite bank of the Avon like a docked liner. A new generation had stopped talking about factories or road-houses, or demanding why the place was not half-timbered or in snow-white marble. Inside, company and audience were on closer terms: the chasm between them had gone and from 1951, in re-modelling, the ends of the circle had been curved round towards the stage. But the quality of performance had to be constant: Hamlet, for the opening of the 1956 Festival, was a classical player of French descent, Alan Badel, known for a strong, confident approach to any part, and his director was Michael Langham: both, Barry Jackson would have said mildly, former Birmingham Repertory men (by now an accolade) just as Olivier had been in the past.

I had hoped that April to return from Stratford with another tale of the power and the glory. Not so: *Hamlet* had no sense of a major occasion. The Prince lay dead; but where was the heart of sorrow as the four captains moved in to bear him like a soldier? We had been bounded in a director's nutshell. All was empty save for an isolated arras that appeared to stand like a furled tent. The background was dead black: lighting alone could build for us from the darkness. Hamlet, in Badel's imagination – he was then thirty-two – was as dolorous a Prince as I could recall. He arrived midway through the first Court scene as if he had had a month of intermittent nightmare and suffered from want of real sleep: a sulky young man who wore a black-trousered ski suit, or possibly battle-dress; when his tunic opened to show a blue shirt he might have been a fireman off-duty. At a *Hamlet* revival we should have no time for wandering irrelevance. We ought not to be caught up, as we were at Stratford, on hearing the King's order before the duel: 'Set me the stoups of wine there beside me.' He could not say 'upon the table' because there was no table, and the mind swung instinctively to *Alice*: 'There were no birds to fly.'

Other people had put Hamlet into a simplified setting and we had considered only the play. But on this spring night, after three and a quarter hours of a very full text, we had lost the tragedy of *Hamlet*. The last four words have been interpreted variously: Matthew Arnold decided that the Prince was 'swayed by a thousand subtle influences, physiological and psychological'. At this remove I am uncertain whether he would have found in Badel's performance much beyond an intelligent young man with a fine torrent of a voice acting away until the sweat stood out on his forehead. Not in itself a bad thing: some actors refrain from acting, and Badel was resolved to taste every speech. Yet all I can recapture now is a rash-embraced despair, centre of a production in a north light so far as there was any light at all: easier, perhaps, to affirm that the revival had the unforgiving north in its spirit. Some speeches Hamlet got across, 'How all occasions' and the Graveyard musing; yet this was not the figure that for three centuries and a half had engaged the world's inquiry and its affection.

Beneath the thundercloud we found what cheer we could. A large, sinister Claudius (Harry Andrews), who would have ruled Denmark less diplomatically than Clunes might have done, brought the play to us in 'My offence is rank'; earlier he had seen the dumbshow from which the King's attention can be discreetly withdrawn: it must have been agreeable for him to have any kind of entertainment, for elsewhere in Elsinore there was little sign of 'heavy-headed revel': as well revel in the tomb of *Aida*. The Queen (Diana Churchill), also watching the dumbshow, gave no hint that the Player Queen (who was a girl) wore a similar dress to her own. Mark Dignam's Ghost, impressive in its barking way, indicated that across the Styx there was little time for punctuation. I reached Elsinore, beyond argument, with George Howe, whose Polonius was feasible as well as garrulous, and during an ambassadorial speech for the Voltimand of David William (who, as Williams, was a former Hamlet at Oxford).

The revival lifted a little in the second half of the night; possibly it was the influence of a salmon-pink carpet that was laid down for the Play, though afterwards rolled up while Hamlet was addressing Rosencrantz and Guilden-stern; almost as if Elsinore had been taken over by the bailiffs. But it was noticeable, at the late-night symposium in the Swan's Nest Hotel after critics had finished their work, that the performance was scarcely mentioned. It ought to have been the night – but I believe now it was in the previous season – when Victor Cookman of *The Times* talked of his favourite St John Hankin's *The New Wing at Elsinore*. In this brief sequel-play Hankin observes that Shakespeare's fifth act leaves the kingdom bereft of King, Queen, and Heir-Presumptive. There is all the material for an acute political crisis. Fortinbras fails to rise to it, whereupon Horatio, being more an antique Roman than a Dane, gets to the throne by a *coup d'état*. Bearing no malice, Fortinbras comes later to stay at Elsinore. We meet them walking as usual upon the 'platform', Fortinbras remarking ' 'Tis bitter cold', and Horatio replying impatiently, 'And you are sick at heart. *I* know.' It seems that the place swarms with ghosts – those of Hamlet's father, Claudius, Gertrude, Ophelia, Rosencrantz and Guildenstern, and Hamlet himself who is in the corridors because, indecisive still, he cannot decide which rooms to take. Question: why Rosencrantz and Guildenstern who were beheaded in England, and not Laertes who was killed at Elsinore? No matter. The development within a few pages is complex and ends with Shakespeare's resolve to haunt the new wing of the castle himself. It is not a fantasy to think of at *Hamlet*, yet it is surprising what can flick into the mind while we sit at the most debated of tragedies.

V

Historians of the stage are accustomed to beginning a new chapter, or new book, at May 1956, a month when the English theatre entered a protracted heatwave. This was after the London production, at the Royal Court, of *Look Back in Anger* by John Osborne, who claimed that the younger generation had a right to feel very angry and said so in an impetuous anecdote. Impetuous or not, it thrust the door open to an outcry of writers who wanted to say much the same thing. It had no effect at the time on any fresh treatment of *Hamlet*.

Escaping from the crush, I was happier to be with a Birmingham Repertory revival of Shaw's *Caesar and Cleopatra*, invited to the International Theatre Festival in Paris: a city so naturally theatrical that professional players could hardly compete with the life of the streets. (A Parisian tramp asleep would be more like a tramp asleep than any rival elsewhere.) The stage for Barry Jackson's cast was at the Sarah-Bernhardt in the Place du Châtelet with its massive red-and-gold auditorium, four tiers rising into shadow; the play had the festival's most generous welcome, surviving even, as a final test, the Quatorze Juillet fireworks. A hardly visible part was acted by a young man named Albert Finney, not long from drama school: one day he would be the English National Theatre's first Hamlet on the South Bank.

No other revivals in 1956, but I returned during October to a placid Stratford to see what might have occurred to its *Hamlet* during the past six months. I had always believed in accepting the immediate first night impression of a performance new-born. But a great deal had to rest on an actor's method: Michael Redgrave, a confessed slow starter – and no discredit to him – regretted that stage history had to be written in premières; he felt that on a last night he could be getting somewhere. Other players (as Eric Keown put it benignly) strike twelve or thirteen at once: the difference between forked lightning and a glint on the horizon.

I was anxious, anyway, to try Stratford again: a town free in October from tourist-hustling, a swan-feathered Avon nearly deserted. Visually, on the bare stage, Badel's Hamlet, living on his nerves, was often closer to Elsinore: we were undistracted by outward shows except by an intermittent fixed stare. He used his voice less prodigally, though he moved me only in a shattering cry of 'Mother!' during the Closet scene. During the year he discovered much in the romantic Berowne of *Love's Labour's Lost* and in Lucio (*Measure for Measure*), a will o'the wisp over the marsh; yet if he had further discoveries in Hamlet he failed to announce them. Maybe they would have emerged – too late, for the season had to end, and I do not think that he returned to the part.

9
WATERLOO ROAD: 1957

THROUGH the 1950s we could count upon an assignation with Shakespeare at the Old Vic, though what we met (an odd *All's Well That Ends Well* for one) was not invariably Shakespearian in mood. These could be exhilarating times in Waterloo Road. The Vic, under Michael Benthall and with a five-year programme to cover every play in the Folio, had long outgrown those early seasons, exciting though some could be, when imagination had to transfigure makeshift. It seemed a world away from nights on which Lilian Baylis, wry and alert, and ready for a sharp word with any offending 'bounder' if something went adrift or was palpably expensive, raked the house from her crimson-draped box: Pryce-Jones called the boxes 'punts laid up for the winter'. Vic regulars, from the gallery down, but particularly in the gallery, guarded their theatre and its players with possessive affection.

They were still doing so by 1957, two decades after Lilian Baylis had died. With Benthall's five-year plan in its final eight or nine months, the Vic had in John Neville, aged thirty-two, the obvious choice for a new Hamlet, the first in Waterloo Road since Richard Burton. Since he joined from Bristol he had played Fortinbras to Burton – new life in shattered Elsinore – and had gone on to almost a score of leading parts. Promptly the gallery had adopted him, an actor of near-Scandinavian fairness, grave and high-cheekboned, his eyes of a very clear blue and his voice a low baritone that could mount to splendour or modulate to an elegiac cadence. The gallery's warmth probably harmed him among people who reacted on principle against popular demonstration, though this was by no means thoughtless fan worship. Most irritated was the young drama critic, Kenneth Tynan, a clever extrovert who at this period wrote for the *Observer*. He made a point of glaring his displeasure at the Vic gallery (which took not the slightest notice) as if it had done him a personal wrong. The ritual over, he would stalk down the aisle like a new Simon Tappertit: 'Something will come of this. I hope it mayn't be human gore.'

Hamlet was the centre of the plan's last year. Benthall, who knew the play as well as any British director, had more to say about it, though his revival would fuel the old cry that critics thought first in comparatives, everyone out to defend a personal view of the tragedy. Hamlet is not a single man but a confederation. On the night of September 18 1957, we found a flat-stage Elsinore with an indeterminate background; the costumes, vaguely Ruritanian, an 'amalgam of nineteenth-century European court dress': nothing expressed in fancy.

Hamlet was revealed standing at one side of the Court, his austere face thin and very white against the 'inky cloak', here a black frogged jacket. In those first minutes he proclaimed the depth of his sorrow: I had no difficulty thereafter in crediting him while he refused to hide the part in fervid vocalising, over-romantic bravura. It was a direct, central performance, a forward drive through a world in wreck. Benthall's scene transposition, based on the First Quarto of 1603, was little remarked, 'To be, or not to be' and the Nunnery scene in the second act instead of the third.

Neville, having 'placed' Hamlet securely, kept a command he would not have lost, whatever the scene order. Dr Muriel St Clare Byrne, writing in the American *Shakespeare Quarterly*, was a voice against change. 'I am more than doubtful,' she said, 'about the wisdom of following the order from the First Quarto, though I can well believe that this is how the play may originally have been acted (but not, *therefore*, constructed). *Hamlet* does not drive ahead like *Macbeth* or *Othello*: it is a play which needs space as well as speed, expansion as well as progression – a movement like the waves of an incoming tide, which fall back after each surge forward, and spread more widely the next time. The scenic order upon which the Second Quarto and the Folio agree makes this the characteristic movement of the play as a whole, and the tension thus created is subtler and more dramatic, with the alternations of depression and exaltation, inertia and energy.'

The players, especially Judi Dench, straight from drama school as a fresh and true Ophelia, were wholly fortifying. Listening to the King and Queen (here Jack Gwillim and Coral Browne), I realised again how in performance down the years Claudius had changed much more than Gertrude. He used merely to be a melodramatically hypocritical King of Spades. Today, however ruthless, he is clearly an effective ruler and diplomatist, and (as Alec Clunes presented him in 1955–56) no coarse usurper unable to hold his Rhenish but still with charm enough for his weak-willed, sensual Queen. Actresses and directors have rarely had second thoughts about Gertrude (even if, once at least, she has been played as an inveterate alcoholic).

I would often see Neville again but never as Hamlet. Without regarding his Vic performance as simply an actor's sierra of peak and valley, I can bring back several passages: his agony ('Remember thee!') after the Ghost's revelation, the unhampered logic of the soliloquies, amused patience with he Gravedigger, the beautifully inflected irony with Osric, the blaze of the duel. He is now a leader of the Canadian stage. We met last, surprisingly, during a symposium on Sarah Bernhardt in Guelph, Ontario, when he slipped into the next seat to listen to a lecture. Today, not far from Guelph, he is directing the Stratford, Ontario, Festival.

II

A famous player who never arrived in Waterloo Road was Frank Benson, paladin of the provinces and Stratford (I doubt whether he would have described Stratford as provincial). He had died at eighty in his Kensington lodgings, sleeping away his life in the fading of the year, on New Year's Eve, 1939. Through much of the late 1950s I was engaged on the biography of a man who looked like the noblest Roman of them all and could have been a Greek in Periclean Athens. Tales of his obsession with sport are still tiresomely exaggerated, a legend (he believed) that started with the most rubbed of the stories when he telegraphed to an actor, 'You must play Rugby', meaning the character in *The Merry Wives of Windsor*. 'No more truth in it than that,' Benson said, though he did regard physical fitness and stamina as important: 'Stanislavsky would have agreed.'

He first played Hamlet as an actor-manager with his own company; previously, with Walter Bentley's company, which he took over, he was Rosencrantz in an appalling straggly yellow wig. At twenty-four he was thinking his way into the part, a Prince who could be tenderness itself but who obviously had the quickest brain in the court of Denmark and would have led a bloody rebellion against Claudius at the drop of a sword. They praised him on tour at Oxford where the *Oxford Magazine*, observing that he avoided Irving's mannerisms, added:

'Great as Mr Irving's genius is, his peculiarities contribute as little to his greatness as do the spots on the sun to its heat. Too many of his disciples reproduce the spots.' In 1886 Benson, and his own mannerisms, was Hamlet at Stratford which in so many ways would be the pivot of his life. Sitting apart, remote and sad, refusing a wine-cup offered to him by a page, he spoke 'A little more than kin and less than kind' in a throbbing voice, harsh in timbre: an inexplicable voice that someone would compare to the note of the telegraph wires but would also have the swirl of Ruskin's 'fluted wave'.

Benson was Hamlet during most of his life. During 1899, at Stratford, he directed the entire Folio text in two instalments, afternoon and evening, startling at a day when older actor-managers sliced and summarised until the tragedy became a verbal steeplechase for the Prince, watched by an assembly of shadows. At this period his own performance, which was never set but shifted its emphases as he felt inclined, suffered from acute melancholia and moved at a tardy pace. When he reached London, at the Lyceum in 1900, A. B. Walkley said in *The Times*: 'This, if not exactly sour, is an *aigre-doux* prince . . . a person, naturally sweet, who finds setting the out-of-joint time right not quite so uncongenial a task as he declares.'

I sought to rescue Benson's career in a multitude of talks with his players, nearly all of whom have died, and in a frenzy of correspondence. This letter came from Basil Rathbone, who joined the company in 1912: 'I was playing Bernardo – and also doubling Guildenstern with a walk-on courtier in the last act. In the opening scene on the parapet of Elsinore, Mr Benson suddenly stopped the rehearsal and asked for a quality in the voice that would show it was night. He asked me if I was not aware of the difference in the quality of one's voice when it was used at night. "You may be enjoying yourself at some party," he said, "and you

walk out of the house into the garden. As you continue to
talk with your companions your voice, almost un-
consciously, changes its quality as the mystery of night
folds its cloak gently about you . . ."'

In the West End of London Benson finally acted Hamlet
at the St Martin's Theatre during 1920: he was sixty-one.
He directed the production in six acts and twelve scenes;
and he ended the play as he usually did, as he would at
Plymouth when he was seventy-two, and as he had in that
Stratford April long before, upon 'The rest is silence.' No
valediction, and no Fortinbras to order the last rites.

10

OUT OF TOWN: 1958–62

I

THE five-year plan in the Old Vic's quick forge and working-house of thought ended during 1958 with *Henry VIII* (Edith Evans as Queen Katharine, John Gielgud as Wolsey). That June, eight years after the New Theatre, Michael Redgrave was in Stratford for his second Hamlet, directed now by Glen Byam Shaw (whose first it was). Everything on the night was set out in the most lucid terms – as it was indeed during that Plymouth *Hamlet* of thirty-six years before from the moment that Barnardo (and Francisco) spoke in their hushed after-dark voices upon the Platform. In the provinces then creative 'production' in the modern sense did not exist; the companies were rehearsed from anxiously assembled stock promptbooks. Even so, each of the performances, 1922 and 1958, put the tragedy upon the stage without blurring it. Agreed, at Plymouth you had to face the day's stereotyping – not that at my age it would have alarmed me. At Stratford you could have taken any stranger to the Memorial Theatre and shown him the tragedy developed like a fastidiously printed text. If you had not met *Hamlet* previously it would have excited you. If you were experienced you might have desired – as I did selfishly – something more theatrically potent, beyond a scholarly exposition, though this put Hamlet's mind like a chart before us; nothing of the super-subtle confusion of the exegetists.

Redgrave's touching and nobly-imagined Prince (he was then fifty) observed all observers. When Rosencrantz and Guildenstern appeared, he fixed them with a look that should have sent them scurrying to their holes. He appeared throughout to be two moves ahead of everyone else, yet, swift though his intuition was, he took longer than in the past to explain it to us. He was dilatory because he had to dissect any phrase, an untiring searcher. From the four hours I recall a harsher edge than to some Hamlets of that period, the full drive of 'O, what a rogue and peasant slave', a haunted whisper behind Claudius at prayer, a second or two of false hope when, alas, it was Polonius that died, and the inevitability of the relaxed acceptance: 'Since no man owes of aught he leaves, what is't to leave betimes?' Aware of Redgrave's power, what he had done with Richard II and the Antony of *Antony and Cleopatra*, triumvir at sunset, it worried me a little not to be wholly with him. I remembered a wistful passage from a lecture he had given at Stratford: 'There are very few English men and women who will venture to shout the accolade, "Bravo!" . . . It does not seem to be in our temperament . . . I know what joy it gives to the performer to have even one voice calling out.'

The production, sets by 'Motley' (Glen Byam Shaw was Gielgud's Laertes in the 'Motley' days of 1934), and costumes after Dürer, was ordered unfussily. It had the bounty of Mark Dignam's King – the actor appeared to be ruling in Elsinore by right – Googie Withers's indolent, doll-like Queen, and Dorothy Tutin, whose Ophelia was a lost child about the castle: more audible than she had been that summer in Verona and Illyria, she went alarmingly mad on a stage turned of a sudden to a staircase. Often, in other productions of the time, the stage appointments alone might have explained Ophelia's madness, but décor now was simple enough: the stage was set principally with gilt and black pillars, with the additions, as required, of escutcheons, candelabra, and the needed properties of a scene: by no means the tragedy of a designer.

Byam Shaw's principal innovation was a Sacristan (Julian Glover) instead of a Second Gravedigger – I had looked for him vainly – a haughty youth more than a little condescending to his senior, the 'goodman delver', and put out at being despatched for a stoup of liquor. For the first time that I could recollect we did not hear of the mysterious Yaughan, who could have been Yohan, keeper of a tavern near the Globe. I liked the Sacristan; a pity that in future revivals we should inevitably be back to the usual stooge. I thought of Sir Cedric Hardwicke (who once startled London by playing the First Gravedigger, First Clown, in modern dress) on a performance he saw, during youth, in a theatre at Stourbridge:

> When the First Gravedigger came to the lines, 'Go, get thee to Yaughan, and fetch me a stoup of liquor', he paused, and then added: 'But stay! I am expecting a gal on a bier.' This raised a big laugh, but the Second Gravedigger got a bigger one and his revenge by making his exit, ostensibly to fetch the stoup of liquor, through the door of the church.

The Sacristan was a change from a character with whom low comedians had had their fun interminably, a kind of village idiot, though he does get in a good jest about the gallows-maker (at which Polonius might have said, 'How pregnant sometimes his replies are! A happiness that often madness hits on . . .'). The author of *Letters of an Unsuccessful Actor*, the late H. A. Saintsbury, wrote of Gomersal, once proprietor of the theatre at Worcester. An actor went along to ask for free admission, and a dialogue ensued:

Manager: What line?

Actor: Second Low Com.

Manager: Is she to be buried in Christian burial that wilfully seeks her own salvation?

Actor: I tell thee she is, and therefore make her grave straight.

Manager: Pass One.

Nowadays there is bad news for the Second Gravedigger (nineteen lines). He is likely to lose his occupation, for we are told that he is only a companion who chances to be around, a stoup-fetcher on whom the older man can try his repository of riddles. It may be long before I can accommodate myself to an anonymous 'Other'; but Professor Harold Jenkins holds that the tradition which makes the second man, as well as the first, a gravedigger, 'goes against the implications of the dialogue' though it dates from the seventeenth century.

II

A few months after this I was in a Birmingham Repertory audience that looked, as it felt, adventurous. Certainly, in those days only Barry Jackson would have dreamt of putting on the night's triple bill, from the morning of the English theatre. It began with the slightest of the three plays, one written in battling couplets and with a title that ribboned out into *A Mery Play Between Johan Johan, the Husbande, Tyb, His Wyfe, and Syr Johan, the Preest*. From 1533–4 and probably the work of John Heywood, former player of the virginals and head of St Paul's singing school, who seemed to have a gift for the 'mery interlude', this could have been the pilot for several instalments of a Tudor cartoon-serial: the triangle of domineering wife, badgered husband (a turning worm) and complacent priest:

a group that might have been referred back to Chaucer. A second, far sterner, choice, the anonymous *A Yorkshire Tragedy* (*c* 1608), dramatising the crimes of a Yorkshire squire, was one of the chosen fourteen of the Shakespeare Apocrypha and unlikely to be more than apocryphal (much better, at least, than *Fair Em, the Miller's Daughter of Manchester*).

It was the third play that mattered most, *Fratricide Punished*. William Poel could not have realised, when he disinterred it during the 1920s, that it would be as funny as it is. It presents, in the flattest prose dialogue, what occurred when English strolling players in Germany at the end of Elizabeth's reign were asked to act the Hamlet play much talked about (maybe the First Quarto?). Having nothing in their repertory, they cheerfully cooked up a script, no doubt from actors in the group who had experienced different versions. This product of composite enthusiasm was translated into German, and what we have now is the German text rendered back into English with a bizarre result. The pomping folk could not be much of a hand with the poetry or philosophy, but they knew that the plot ought to serve. It did, and does. What we saw that night in Birmingham was the reduction of the tragedy to swift bathos; the Ghost boxing the sentry's ear; the weather not 'bitter cold' but 'not so cold as it was'; jamming of the soliloquies into a few nonchalant lines; such friendly exchanges as 'O, sir, there's a ghost here which appears every quarter of an hour' – 'There is some mystery in this'; a rapid telescoping of events; Ophelia's floral dance (at the end the poor girl falls from a high hill off-stage); matter-of-fact realism from the Queen, 'If the Pope had not allowed the marriage, it would never have taken place'; the King's explanatory 'I hope that when they both drink of the wine they will then die'; and his unctuous 'I deserve my evil fate.' In the most notorious scene, the Prince – acted by

Mark Kingston with happy fervour – dropped strategically to the ground at the right moment, allowing a pair of Pirates to shoot each other across him. Whereupon he observed, 'O just Heaven, praise be to thee ever for this angelic idea!' We could remember how Shakespeare's Bastard Faulconbridge in *King John* applauded the device by which 'From north to south Austria and France shoot in each other's mouth'.

It had been an angelic idea of Jackson's; adventurous or not, the company during the triple bill played to fifty-eight per cent of the theatre's capacity. In the following year, 1959, *Fratricide Punished* went up to the Edinburgh Festival, preceded there by an early sunlit cock-crow of the stage, *Gammer Gurton's Needle*, a bucolic farce (or 'a right pithy, pleasant and merrie comedie') by a 'university dramatist' known as Master S, that had set audiences laughing when Shakespeare was still a boy. *Fratricide* was the same resolute skirmish, Mark Kingston's Hamlet even more determined and his colleagues keeping faces straight and prose blunt. 'I will so avenge myself,' Hamlet says hopefully, 'on this ambitious, murderous, and adulterate man that ever afterwards posterity shall talk of it – now will I go and, feigning madness, wait until I find a time to effect my revenge.' A Scots voice near me whispered, 'Are there not uncommon twists?' On the whole, yes; there were.

Bernard Hepton directed with gentle ease. I could not help thinking that, on such an occasion as this, there could have been room for that pompous old Victorian John Coleman's instruction to a super at rehearsal (but not of *Fratricide*): 'My dear sir, when you ascend the raking piece and leave the stage, be good enough to emit a greasy laugh of truculent defiance.'

III

A member of the 1958–9 Birmingham company, Ian

Richardson, would go on to be acknowledged, especially at Stratford (where he played Richard II, Coriolanus, Iachimo, Pericles, and much else), as among the first of current classical actors; a prominent career in television followed. At Birmingham he was in his salad days. 'Let us impart what we have seen tonight unto young Hamlet,' says Horatio; and it was a very youthful Prince (Richardson was just on twenty-four) that moved through the castle mazes: no mature leader of the stage after a packed life of theatre-craft. This accorded with Barry Jackson's belief that nobody over thirty should appear as Hamlet or any of his contemporaries; if a Hamlet had to be over thirty then he should look younger and certainly be young at heart. The age has been assumed on the strength of the Gravedigger's assertion: 'I came to 't that day . . . that young Hamlet was born . . . I have been sexton here, man and boy, thirty years.' (Yet, at the beginning of the play, in I.2, Hamlet contemplates going back to university in Wittenberg.)

In the mind he remains 'young Hamlet'. During the spring of 1959, environed by the shades of so many actors before him, Richardson fought against his audiences' knotted and combined memories, and remarkably succeeded. In Hepton's production, keeping the play in an undistorted mirror, the dilemma of idealistic, baffled youth, Hamlet entered as a slight, sad-eyed figure of settled melancholy, a young man's single-minded sorrow. At that hour Richardson's personality had yet to develop. What would become a magnificent voice needed range, the larger theatrical passion, but the actor's earnestness and sweetness achieved much. If it was not the work of a virtuoso seeking to be by turns all that Hamlet is, a man of 'insoluble opposites', from the end of the Ghost scene it grasped the imagination. We knew that this was one of the many Hamlets in that multiplex creation: Richardson had the words and the questing mind. Though, unluckily, he did not play the part again, I doubt whether he could have recalled just that stricken boyishness. In a 'short' text of more than three hours, he – or Barry Jackson perhaps – chose a few of Dr Dover Wilson's readings ('How express and admirable in action'). Some of the cuts surprised me, the Ghost's 'And duller shouldst thou be', Hamlet's 'And shall I couple hell?', and (I was sorry about this) 'He has my dying voice.'

IV

Unlike W. A. (Bill) Darlington of the *Daily Telegraph*, who could tell me regularly of discoveries he had made over most of England, I had rarely been to school plays; once or twice to Harrow, Repton, Denstone, and the Sloane School, but not often enough to bring back sustained impressions, and only twice to a *Hamlet*. The first, treasure for any collector, was in a line of annual productions at King Edward's High School for Girls in Birmingham, fortunate to have an English mistress, Kate Flint, who cared anxiously for the performance of Shakespeare. Her girls at various times included Ellen Dryden, who was Hermione in *The Winter's Tale* and would be an accomplished dramatist, and in *Romeo and Juliet* (as the Nurse) the future Jonsonian scholar, Dr Rosalind Miles.

The *Hamlet* night lingers, my first and so far my only female Prince: not an experiment to try too often (though Frances de la Tour was praised at a London fringe theatre, the Half Moon, during the 1980s). The Nunnery and Closet scenes must be awkward, whatever the actress's sensibility. I was too young for Alice Marriott, who was Edgar Wallace's paternal grandmother; or Clare Howard, who was 'addicted to music cues', illustrative 'chords' and 'crashes'; or Mrs Bandmann-Palmer, who worked generally on the circuits of the manufacturing North, and who off-stage wore tweeds and hob-nailed boots and had an insensate passion for watercress at all times. She is said to have acted Hamlet with some melodramatic force, though because of rheumatism she had trouble in rising from her knees. Moreover, I did not see in 1899, and in a contentious prose version, the player Max Beerbohm called 'Hamlet, Princess of Denmark': Sarah Bernhardt in a highly-coloured portrait of a young man of unclouded intellect. (Several years earlier she had cast herself as Ophelia with no special response.) After reporting that Bernhardt's Hamlet, if neither melancholy nor a dreamer, was at least someone of consequence and unmistakably thoroughbred, Max could provide only an ambiguous compliment: that the Prince was, from first to last, *une très grande dame*. She was the sole woman Hamlet in Stratford history. Critics less ironical than Max had spoken of her as an always practical personage who realised the magnitude of Hamlet's task and his danger. There were important voices on her behalf, if not that of *Punch* which, with a moderately straight face, nominated Henry Irving as Ophelia.

Far indeed in time, place and manner from King Edward's School: there, in a sensibly straight production, it was sometimes affecting to hear the play through the minds of its young actresses, particularly Marion McNaughton's Hamlet, a figure of haunted grace ready for any diversity of mood. It was, as I told Bill Darlington, eager for news from the front line, a night unimpeded by dagger and asterisk and offering the sound with the sense. During the next summer, 1960, I saw at Solihull School, established farther down in Warwickshire four years before Shakespeare's birth, an hour of my only boy Hamlet. It had to be a production in the making; but Christopher Thompson's 'darkly shining' voice – he was cast before he had acted anything at all – hinted that he could have won a fellowship in a cry of players. We were asked, generally, to view

Hamlet in the Elizabethan light of Bertram Joseph's *Conscience and the King*, remembering that by the aristocratic code of honour the Prince must take revenge on Claudius, but that if he were to obey only a devil in his father's shape, then the killing must lead to the horrors of damnation. Little at Solihull, I think, would have surprised Shakespeare. 'Do the boys carry it away?' – 'Ay, that they do, my lord.'

By 1961 Peter Hall, thirty-year-old successor to Byam Shaw as the youngest administrator in Stratford record – one day he would direct the National Theatre – had settled down at the Memorial: he renamed this the Royal Shakespeare Theatre and he arranged for a first London base (primarily then for modern plays) at the Aldwych. From the beginning it was clear, with by-ways of experiment to be explored, that he would not stick to the high road. Within a few years he and his collaborator, John Barton, formerly a Cambridge don (like several theatre-men at the time, Hall had a Cambridge background) would bring to Stratford the three Parts of *Henry VI* as an elaborately re-jigged trilogy, *The Wars of the Roses*.

The first *Hamlet* (1961) of the new Stratford order was directed by Peter Wood, also a former Cambridge man and a little older than Hall. His production, in retrospect a mingling of careful thought and superficiality, reached us in three movements. A first ended not at the 'Rogue and peasant slave' soliloquy but on the King's 'Madness in great ones must not unwatched go'; a second took us to 'How all occasions', and a third from the Mad scene to the last words of Fortinbras. Wood adopted the First Quarto in making 'To be, or not to be' the second soliloquy, though unlike Benthall in the John Neville *Hamlet* at the Vic, he did not transpose the Nunnery scene also. Farther in the night the plotting of Claudius and Laertes was removed to the graveyard after the burial, a not overtly conspiratorial plan that had become common form. These things helped the run of the narrative, and the director had been reasonable with cuts; as 'short' versions go, and this one took more than three hours-and-a-half, it was fully workable. It did not cling to fashionable readings: I noticed, mildly curious, that after his line about the decaying effect of water on dead bodies, the Gravedigger (who had the moulded-rubber features of an inventive comedian, Newton Blick) spatch-cocked in the First Quarto phrase, ' 'Tis a great soaker'. The night, as I recall it, was pictorial: Leslie Hurry's set, with autumnal curtains, shadowy spaces, and fragmentary 'details'; Elizabethan dress; the opening, a single gleam upon Francisco's helmet in a far corner, and the rest of the 'platform' in dead midnight gloom; the Play scene, with dumbshow, beneath the flare of a candelabrum; and a moment when Hamlet, after leaving his mother's closet, was surrounded by a sword-point ring of bright steel. Early speeches had a strained tautness that summoned the heart-in-mouth atmosphere of that winter night.

All that the director was doing helped the play along as a good story. But the tragedy of Hamlet, Prince of Denmark? For twenty minutes or so I had hoped that Hamlet might be a performance for record. Ian Bannen phrased fluently; grief in the first soliloquy sounded genuine. Then doubt supervened. The voice wanted music and it wanted variety: nothing yet of airs from heaven or blasts from hell. Scene by scene, it was apparent that the night was emerging as a strong narrative rather than high tragedy. Bannen's tones began to hit a note perilously like the soughing of wind in the wires. The sense of grief had gone; once a wailing Ghost had shocked Hamlet into awareness, the young man grew positively resilient. Perhaps he had had an 'antic disposition' at Wittenberg where he would have spoken occasionally in the Union and his friends would have gone round shaking their heads over his neurosis, a man from a failing dynasty.

To our astonishment, when the Players had gone to be well bestowed and he was left to 'O, what a rogue and peasant slave' – a tragedian's full drive – he saw the property-trunk, threw aside the few costumes it contained, jumped into it, the kind of receptacle fit elsewhere for Iachimo, and began the speech as if he were a boy playing with a hip-bath. At his peak, and crying 'O vengeance!' in a spurt of frenzy, he let the lid fall back upon him like an extinguisher. Thereupon he raised it, exclaiming 'O, what an ass am I!' Obviously it had been decided to do something different – words that have damaged so much acted Shakespeare – and to vary the theatrical business in which Hamlet stabs at the King's empty throne. (This happened instead after the Play.) The new business failed to work; it reduced Hamlet's stature, and it would attach itself to memories of the production which somebody wrote off meanly as a trunk murder. Shaw said relentlessly back in 1900: 'If in playing Hamlet you do one ridiculous thing, your Hamlet will be called ridiculous.'

Away from this bad dream, Bannen, a valiant theatre-man, continued to have his moments: the quietness of his interpolations during the Play; his 'Leave me, *friends*!' before the Closet scene; inflections (one a pause on the word 'eggshell' in 'How all occasions') which showed that the lines were sharp in his mind. Yet the performance had to slip towards monotony: we had to regret it because Bannen was often extremely likeable, he could assume a fine romantic pose as when he listened to the First Player (Tony Church), and more than once a speech came over faultlessly unblurred. An obdurate King and brittle Queen (Noel Willman and Elizabeth Sellars) were as believable as anyone; the Ghost's revelation, as Gordon Gostelow uttered it, could stream on the night-wind; but though Geraldine McEwan toiled with Ophelia, her characteristic voice, like another poet's line about the first pipe of half-awakened birds, could here betray her purpose.

v

My next out-of-town *Hamlet*, at the Oxford Playhouse, was less disturbing, a statement from a reliable, matter-of-fact textbook. When its information had been imparted, I was not very anxious to hear it again, even if, in the event, I did so in London a month later, at the Strand Theatre, and recognised that Frank Hauser had been more helpful than some other directors who are governed by a persistent whim. The performance on a stage almost bare remained nevertheless an accurate diagram rather than a living experience. Two players, Linda Gardner's overwhelmed Ophelia and, in London, the Polonius of Robert Eddison, paternally politic, were both newly thought; and Hamlet himself was a pleasant actor, Jeremy Brett.

Agate said in his 1937 obituary of Ion Swinley, the theatre's lamented might-have-been from between the wars, that he had almost everything a romantic player needed: height, appearance, a noble, flexible voice. Brett had height, appearance, and a deep flexible voice. What he did not have, and Swinley did, was any splendour of personality; more correct than many Hamlets, he failed to persuade me as they had done. We understood his suffering; we knew that he possessed some of the qualities Ophelia named; and nothing made me wish to rise and tell the world. What evaded me, as too frequently, was the simple quiver of excitement the play must have. Hamlet could have been a man at the next restaurant table. A good restaurant, but not Hamlet.

I I

INTERLUDE BY THE DANUBE: 1963

I

THANKS to the British Council during the spring of 1963 I was able to see how uncommonly Shakespeare had been acclimatised beside the Danube: the Swan of Danube, if you wish, but no one in Hungary, I was glad to find, talked condescendingly of 'the Bard'. My wife and I found ourselves in Budapest in the very clear, icy light of a late-March morning, wondering how *Hamlet* would fare that evening at the Mádach Theatre. Hungarians regard Shakespeare as their adopted poet, for no other reason than their love of the language which has been translated with extraordinary finesse. As we discovered then, and on later visits, the lovers are articulate. Not more than ten minutes after our aircraft had touched down in mid-evening at Ferihegy airport and we were driving from the suburb towards Budapest, our companion began to talk of Shakespeare. He was still talking of plays and translators when we whisked by the glitter of the river bank lights – ice-blocks were drifting down-stream – and stopped by the hotel door on the Buda side of the broad grey Danube.

Hamlet on the following night would be in the text of the nineteenth-century poet, János Arany, the man from whom Hungarian enthusiasm for Shakespeare had its chief impetus. Though the next two weeks would contain so much else that was non-Shakespearian, it was sensible to begin with *Hamlet*. Elsewhere the dramatist had often suffered from maladroit renderings – in a Spanish *Hamlet* Francisco's ' 'Tis bitter cold and I am sick at heart' arrived as 'It is very cold and I have a weak chest' – but we gathered that there was nothing of this in Hungary where an intricate language had been wedded to Shakespeare's with care and justice. As even a stranger can discern, it is capable of astonishing effects: we realised this when, startled by cadences in the Tomb scene of *Romeo and Juliet*, we asked the translator, Dezsö Mészöly, to analyse his work. Though the plays continue to challenge fresh versions, the few by Arany are regarded as sovereign, threaded into the people's lives. We could not escape from Shakespeare. At, of all things, an American farce, *Harvey*, we heard that its director had smoothed a tiresome passage by an allusion to A *Midsummer Night's Dream* which a Hungarian audience would pick up without question.

Hamlet was the first of the plays put directly into Hungarian, in a 1790 version by Ferencz Kazinczy. But it was Arany's, seventy years later, that established itself as the gold: the newest revival had been for twelve months in the Mádach repertory, and the house listening to it was rapt and crowded. All the main Budapest theatres are in Pest, the metropolitan area, so for playgoing, if you live among the low hills of Buda where the villas are scattered and spaced in mellow beauty, you must cross the Danube. Going to *Hamlet* at dusk, we went by the Margaret Bridge, embankment lights in flower on each side of the river and the Parliament, a neo-Gothic range with a dome un-expectedly added, standing out like a detailed stage back-cloth.

On this visit we saw nine or ten plays (Shakespeare, Shaw, Tennessee Williams, Gogol, O'Neill), but nothing to compare with *Hamlet* in the dignity of the Mádach. In

London we had been passing through a phase of starkness that would minimise a production dangerously. László Vámos, the *Hamlet* director, had set the tragedy upon a wide acreage of platform stage against a high semi-circular wall, massively embossed, that could remind me of Elsinore's Kronborg. Against the wall, a permanent set, pierced as required by niches, arcades, windows, and transformed by lighting acutely evocative, we saw one of the most striking *Hamlet*s in recent memory. Its company worked with tireless technique, led by Miklós Gábor, a man fair-haired, of medium height and then in his mid-thirties; virile, authoritative and supple, with an unchecked command of the vocal line. Some players seem only to be ministering to a mind diseased: Gábor's Prince was a man still young who, knowing too well what he had to do, dreaded its execution and asked for our confidence in his pressing doubts. He was a major Hamlet, whether responding brokenly to a majestic Ghost; arguing through the soliloquies; rising to anger after the Play when his passion flamed like the torches in the later 'Hide, fox' scurry; or meditative in the first Graveyard calm. (Here, but he melted away early, on his errand to Yaughan, was a beguiling Second Low Com.)

We all talked of *Hamlet*. One afternoon, after I had spoken to university students on Shakespeare in the theatre, somebody asked me how Gábor compared with what sounded like Olivia Lawrence. Dimly, not recalling the actress and vaguely puzzled by the context, it took me a minute to recover; the questioner had merely followed the charming Hungarian habit of reversing surname and first name. On another day, after mid-morning black coffee (and apricot brandy), a hospitable professor began to talk of *Hamlet*'s sheer theatrical sweep: 'Yes . . . those first words. The platform before the castle, night and darkness and frost, and the soldier speaking, his voice shaking a little,

"*Ki az?*" ' He went on, and there was hardly any need for our indefatigable interpreter, Lili Halápy, to translate.

One year we would see Gábor as Richard III. Later still there was a *Hamlet* with another player, sincere like his colleagues, but without the personal magnetism that transfigured the first Mádach night: Prince of Denmark, and Prince of Hungary. It is extraordinary that to this day Gábor has never acted in London.

The second Hungarian Hamlet (Peter Huszti), also at the Mádach, years afterwards, with another director, was a romantic: none the worse for that at an hour when a romantic was under-prized, yet seldom an actor who quickened the spirit, left one debating: he was most credible with the Players, a very small troupe, including (as at Stratford in 1956) a young actress, a quirk of casting that would have been odd in 1600. Any memory of *Hamlet*, as years pass, must be a palimpsest of revisions and interlineations; this revival stirred me more on the night than it would next morning. I had again to mourn the loss of Fortinbras. Sam Weller's words would have served: 'It's over, and can't be helped, and that's one consolation as they always says in Turkey when they cuts the wrong man's head off.' I did not try the quotation on anyone in Budapest; somebody without question would have recognised it.

12
NATIONAL: 1963–64

I

'WE should greet the National Theatre with our trumpets and our shawms' said Dame Sybil Thorndike in one of her unforgettable volleys of enthusiasm. She was speaking on the last night of an Old Vic production – the play was *Measure for Measure*, and offstage the bells of Vienna were ringing – the last night, indeed, of an Old Vic company in its Waterloo Road theatre. This was on a June evening in 1963; it would be four months to reopening as the National, though whether that occasion was scored for shawms I cannot hazard. Debate about the new adventure, what exactly should happen and how, might well have begun in the reign of Ethelred the Unready. Our main comfort was the choice of Laurence Olivier as first director, for if anybody could get on with the job while this committee or the other grumbled into its minute-books, he must be the man. It was a relief on October 22 to enter a theatre that, after reconstruction, still wore its past like a robe.

For years the Old Vic had been, in effect, a National Theatre without portfolio (Lilian Baylis would never have argued about the description). Waiting there before curtain-rise on Olivier's production of *Hamlet*, it was natural to think of other times: Charles Laughton's Angelo, a shivering glance at a cankered mind; Maurice Evans's Richard II declaiming 'We are amazed' from the walls of

Flint Castle; Edith Evans, goddess of a Watteau Arden; Sybil Thorndike and Laurence Olivier in Roman grandeur during the Supplication from *Coriolanus*; Gielgud's Lear, bred closely with Granville-Barker; Neville's progress to the captains and the kings. Now a *Hamlet* – fifth I had seen in this building – before a roll-call of the English theatre and upon a stage that for a decade would be national in credit as in name.

At curtain-rise light rested first upon Francisco at his watch, standing upon a ramp, in rough-hewn stone, that strode up across the stage towards the arch of the rebuilt proscenium. The sentry climbed until he was out of sight. Then Barnardo appeared at the foot of the slope, silent before his sudden breath-caught cry – the voice was Richard Hampton's – 'Who's there?', and Francisco's challenge from above: 'Nay, answer me. Stand and unfold yourself.' It was obvious soon that Olivier, as director, must have the night's laurel: this was a production, unhampered in pace, that got through a practically full text in something like four and a half hours. Visually, we were held by a set that Sean Kenny, its designer, had described officially as 'a single piece of thrusting stone curving up to a sharp vertical rock tower. The tower breaks the force of the rising stone and holds it firm. The tower is the throne and the bedhead and the church and alters its position to the ramp to become these things.' Henry Irving or Beerbohm Tree would not have accepted this for a dumbfounded minute, but we did. Looking back at that birth-night, I remember the mounting of the haunted ramparts; the sight of Hamlet, his back against the tower, as he spoke the marking-time 'dram of eale' speech high over the stage; Fortinbras, his back to us, on the sunlit tower while below him Hamlet uttered the soliloquy in which Olivier had once been so masterful, 'How all occasions do inform against me / And spur my dull revenge'; and Ophelia as she rushed out in her madness, preparing to hurl herself from the edge.

These things exist now rather than the acting of Hamlet himself (Peter O'Toole), decidedly a man apart. If in repose he could look bafflingly like late-Victorian photographs of Sir George Alexander in the civilised serenity of Orlando, he was not often in repose. I kept thinking of the King's phrase, 'Like the hectic in my blood he rages', and asking why the passion was barely more than external, seldom inflammable. What I wanted most was another voice; this one could be abrasive and metallic, especially when the tone was forced. I listened and watched without emotion except in the Closet where Hamlet suggested a marked Oedipus complex. Doubtless the performance might have been likened to Sean Kenny's 'single piece of thrusting stone' but it seems far off now and out of reach. I can recover with far less reserve a group of other players: not maybe Max Adrian's Polonius (a part said to have been based on Lord Burghley) whose assemblage of comic fidgets was debatable, but unquestionably Michael Redgrave, devious yet naturally regal as Claudius; Diana Wynyard's sensual, foolish Gertrude, a Queen who, as Eileen Herlie did in the film, drank deliberately from the poisoned cup; Anthony Nicholls, looking, as I am certain the Ghost must look, like something uncoffined; and Rosemary Harris's defeated Ophelia. Her Mad scene, in the view of the actor-critic Robert Speaight, 'far from turning "hell itself to favour and to prettiness", revealed a fury of sexual frustration working on a nature too delicate to sustain the double shock of her father's death and Hamlet's repudiation.' Passages of magnificence, yet I left the theatre unfulfilled and dubious about some of Hamlet's speaking. In *The Dark Lady of the Sonnets* the Beefeater says to Shakespeare, 'What manner of thing is a cadence, sir? I have not heard of it.' Shakespeare replies (and Shaw knew the true answer): 'A thing to rule the world with.' It was Ernest Milton who, late in life and

talking with his strange detached gentleness, said quietly: 'I
think the dove must descend, and sometimes it does.' I
doubt whether, at the Vic that night, the dove descended
upon O'Toole.

II

It would have been an angelic idea – the *Fratricide* phrase
creeps in – if the first European Hamlet at the National had
been Miklós Gábor. As it was, the visitors were from Italy,
about a year after the theatre had opened and when
excitement was waning a little from the Olivier Othello.
Practically a decade earlier he had told an interviewer that
he kept off this part because it wanted 'a great blue-black
voice'; splendidly he invented the voice and triumph
followed. That was in Shakespeare's quatercentenary
spring. During the September of 1964 the Italian *Hamlet*, a
prose text, was staged by the Proclemer-Albertazzi
company, directed by Franco Zeffirelli, a man who, like
Tyrone Guthrie in Britain (and later in most places on the
map), had to be met upon his hour. Zeffirelli's Vic *Romeo
and Juliet* could be incautiously praised, but nobody denied
that its world was Verona. *Othello* (Stratford, 1961) was
miscast. He would have fun at the National with an edited
English text of *Much Ado About Nothing*, in the poly-
chromatic brouhaha of twentieth-century Sicily. But first
his Italian *Amleto* where the merits were principally
atmospheric. After four hours we recalled a nearly empty
stage of misty depths, a range of lights in varied intensity
above it (the chiaroscuro could be daring), and the players
seeming at times to rise from the cauldron mouth of a
circular aperture down-stage. Here, in a very full Italian
text, was a contemporary Hamlet, a young man-of-the-
world of exceedingly high voltage, wearing jeans and a
charcoal sweater and seeking to pierce and defy the barriers

of convention. Giorgio Albertazzi was wholly a Hamlet of
the defiant 1960s when all had to be keyed to the mood of a
Polish scholar's programme note: 'What matters is that,
through Shakespeare's text, we ought to get at our modern
experience, anxiety, and sensibility.' The writer was
Professor Jan Kott.

During the performance, verbal magic dissipated,
suspense did not slacken. The cast acted with trained
vigour, every movement intensified. You might see every-
day counterparts any morning in any Tuscan town,
lavishing on the mildest chat a wealth of gesture and a
fantastic prodigality of intonation. I was not satisfied that
we got from this production, unremittingly florid, all that
Zeffirelli expected us to get: 'The conflict between man's
twin natures, the divine and the diabolical, with all the
significance and evolution of those two primordial
elements of good and evil.' Better to have described it as a
relishing outbreak of the theatre theatrical: such matters as
the midnight colloquy on the ramparts, the First Player
rolling out his Trojan speech like the clamour of a thunder-
sheet, Hamlet debating 'To be, or not to be' in agonised
soliloquy from a spiral stair within the cauldron mouth, and
flinging Ophelia across the stage in the Nunnery scene; the
elaboration of the dumbshow, the frenzy of the Closet;
Ophelia's uninhibited dementia, a tempest of the mind (she
was Annamaria Guarnieri); and the sudden chill of the
graveyard. The night comes back as a kind of furious
shadow dance. Anna Proclemer's Gertrude was a decorative shell of a woman whose hair had gone white after
the Closet scene; the King (Massimo Girotti) was coolly
sophisticated, and Mario Scaccia a Polonius bulkily bourgeois. Mark Twain said, in effect, of an ambiguous
beverage, 'It was only fair coffee, but I'd call it very good tea.'
That could have been the word for this sultry production, not
really a major *Hamlet* but a very good *Amleto*.

III

For me that Italian tumult at the Vic could have appeared noisier than it was because, a few months earlier, I had seen the most modest of footnotes to the Shakespeare quatercentenary: *Hamlet* put on by as regarded an amateur company as any in the provinces, the Crescent Theatre of Birmingham. It was so uncomplicated that when its director, Edwin Lilley, resolved to spring an unalarming thunderstorm in the Graveyard scene, I assumed involuntarily that it must be mentioned in some obscure cranny of the text. (With Zeffirelli it would have been Lear's storm on the heath, doubled and redoubled.) The director's note was clear: a play 'on the grand scale about a group of people who are destroyed, and who cause each other's destruction, because they are corrupted by the evil which encircles them.'

During a sensible night the Hamlet (Norman Cockin) was happiest in the lower notes, the calmer passages. If I was less happy about a Ghost who appeared at first to be reading the minutes of the last meeting, buried Denmark has never been the simplest of personages. Only a pedant would have questioned the arrival (yet again) of an actress in the strolling company. I liked very much the decision not to cut the complete Hamlet-Horatio scene (V.2) that in a short text can frequently begin at 'But I am very sorry, good Horatio, that to Laertes I forgot myself.' Always I have wished to have the full description of Hamlet stealing from his cabin in the dark, his sea-gown scarf'd about him, fingering the royal packet, returning to open in private the 'grand commission' that ordered his instant execution, and to devise a new one in which the bearers should be put to sudden death, no shriving-time allow'd. It is a part of the story that we have to hear and listening at the Crescent I wondered how directors can ever justify a cut. It was strange that Zeffirelli did not put it all into mime, and the ensuing sea-fight into the bargain.

IV

We have always expected something different from a new Hamlet; but it is only in fairly recent years that Ophelia and the Ghost have changed. My first Ophelia, in 1922, was a young woman who in aspect could have been the ingénue of a genteel comedy. She spoke 'O, what a noble mind is here o'erthrown' as if she were reading an obituary from the local paper, and when her own mind was overthrown she followed the tradition of all well-brought-up girls. She wore a wreath, carefully adjusted. She carried a florist's posy of rosemary, pansies, fennel, columbines, and rue; she sang discreetly in tune and occasionally, according to the rubric, spoke things in doubt that carried but half sense. Presently she left to become (in the Queen's speech) an Academy picture by Millais. Not that every actress was like this – one had only to name, with a lapse of years between them, Ellen Terry and Fay Compton – but there was a routine mad-girl act that for years audiences, inured to it, accepted without comment. It would be a shock when, in our post-war theatre, Ophelia began to go genuinely mad, no conventional charade but the picture of a broken mind, divided from herself and her fair judgment, tragedy's helpless victim, her singing a cry from the darkness: sights and sounds to evoke her brother's 'O heat, dry up my brains, tears seven times salt / Burn out the sense and virtue of mine eye!' More actresses were thinking independently, searching for new ways to express a set-piece that for so long seemed to have been grafted on to the play, not a terrifying part of the narrative. Early Ophelias, says Professor Arthur Colby Sprague, were likely to carry straws (she spurned 'enviously at straws') and make play with a scarf or veil. Sprague records: 'Ellen Terry always had real flowers – "no matter what the cost" – and perhaps, under pre-Raphaelite influence, carried in 1883 "a lily branch in her hand". After that, of course, one hears no more about straws.'

A demented girl was one matter in frenzied Elsinore. But what of the Ghost, a dead and loquacious King who walks his own battlements in full armour, a marshal's truncheon in his hand, his beard a sable silver'd:

> What art thou that usurp'st this time of night,
> Together with that fair and warlike form
> In which the majesty of buried Denmark
> Did sometimes march?

What indeed? The English drama is heavily haunted. As a rule, Elizabethan/Jacobean spectres were grimly sepulchral: massive citizens of the other world, from a neo-Senecan revenge-and-slaughter school in the manner of Andrea, Thomas Kyd's Spaniard (*The Spanish Tragedy*) or Webster's Brachiano (*The White Devil*): 'Enter Ghost in his leather cassock and breeches, bootes, a coule; in his hand a pot of lilly-flowers with a scull in't.' But none would be so eloquent as Hamlet's father, even if during a traditional haunting we have sometimes wished that the too, too solid flesh would melt, thaw and resolve itself into a dew. It is no good to be emptily sonorous, though through history the routine Ghost has boomed on towards the dawn. An actor must persuade us that he has risen from the depths to relate his story to his son before returning 'to fast in fires / Till the foul crimes done in my days of nature / Are burnt and purged away'. Bernard Shaw, who held that the part was a wonder of the tragedy, and who demanded the next-to-impossible, spoke of 'the weird music of that long speech which should be the spectral wail of a soul's bitter wrong crying from one world to another in the extremity of its torment'.

Yet how to present the Ghost at a time when, 'weird music' or not, few people will accept the supernatural, let alone so dominant a phantom as this? Further, not many stage Ghosts suggest that they believe in themselves: one rare exception, we are told, was the actor Courtenay Thorpe early in the century, and in the Barrymore revival at the Haymarket during 1925. It is not enough for Hamlet to be affrighted, whatever Garrick was according to the German traveller Lichtenberg in 1775:

> At these words [Horatio's 'Look, my lord, it comes'] Garrick turns sharply and at the same moment staggers back two or three paces with his knees giving way under him; his hat falls to the ground and both his arms, especially the left, are stretched out nearly to their full length, with the hands as high as his head, the right arm more bent and the hand lower, and the fingers apart; his mouth is open: thus he stands rooted to the spot, with legs apart, but no loss of dignity, supported by his friends.

(I have never been able to take this detailed description quite seriously.)

In these days, after the Ghost's emergence – maybe through a mist; traditionally it would rise from a trap-door – an actor should play it with as much dignity as possible and rely upon the quality of voice. Various Hamlets during the last fifty years have taken the speeches themselves, not the happiest form of filial duty. Raymond Massey described in *A Hundred Different Lives* how Norman Bel Geddes, who directed his Hamlet in New York as far back as 1931 – and who cut the text to two and a half hours – fired the Ghost after a few days' rehearsal. In consequence, Massey found himself speaking the lines to a 'a floating, silent, disembodied head. Some of the traditionalists became cardiac cases at the blasphemy but some customers actually liked it.' Other directors since those carefree Broadway nights have continued to like the 'Freudian trick' – one that Olivier used in his film – but it is a dubious way of getting round a part (about ninety lines in full text, seventy in the 'short') that is said to have been the top of Shakespeare's own performance. Jonathan Pryce employed this at the Royal Court in 1980; instead of seeing the Ghost (as we presume Horatio and Marcellus did) he was possessed by it and spoke in tones that sounded at least three-parts throttled.

13

STUDENT PRINCE: 1965–69

I

IMPELLED by the vigour and prophetic imagination of
Peter Hall, Stratford had been rediscovering (but more
elaborately than Jackson had done at Birmingham) the
three parts of *Henry VI*. These were put together during
1963, the whole trilogy, now freshly divided as *The Wars of
the Roses*, sharpened to what in another context had been
called 'a spire of meaning' and brought into a compass of
five and three quarter hours. John Barton, the Royal
Shakespeare Company's specialist scholar, who edited the
text with its battles, sieges, fortunes, an entire armoured
division, had a complex duty in transposing, telescoping,
and, a matter for which he had enviable talent, composing
lines, sometimes whole scenes of bridging pastiche ('Now,
by my youth and by my hallow'd crown, / I will uphold my
conscience and my will'). Barton was above the skirmish of
previous Shakespeare adapters, hit-or-miss. Hall, explain-
ing reason and method in a preface to the published texts,
quoted an anonymous fumbler with a *Hamlet* which
survived for some years after Irving: he was before my
time. Certainly a man without the Barton expertise, he
ended the play thus: 'Goodnight, sweet prince, / And
flights of angels sing thee to thy rest / Whilst I remain
behind to tell a tale / That shall hereafter make the hearers
pale.' And probably did.

The Wars of the Roses, an imperious success, proved to be a good time for the twenty-two-year-old actor of Henry, a man fitter for monkish tonsure than the English crown. David Warner progressed in 1964 to Richard II. There he was cast less securely, having to compete, except for younger people, with memories of Gielgud, Hayes and Redgrave, Maurice Evans and John Neville, all masters of the spoken word. Warner's tone was either mellifluous or mumbled: the part needed a sharper definition, but when he wished (not invariably) his Richard could be conscious of the verse. Peter Hall, who had faith in him, saw him as the right casting for a new Hamlet and this production in August 1965, the actor's third Stratford season, would be argued about for years.

Less than twelve months before, Giorgio Albertazzi had been playing his Italian prose Hamlet at the National and quoting Professor Jan Kott, who then ruled Shakespearian thinking in the theatre. He was the author of a debated book, deriving from the woes of his nation, in which he saw Shakespeare as a contemporary and interpreted the plays to square with this view. Peter Brook had been profoundly influenced by him in directing *King Lear* (Kott's essay was entitled '*King Lear* or *Endgame*'). Peter Hall had believed in 'the direct contemporary relevance of the *Henry VIs*'. Kott described A *Midsummer Night's Dream* as a candid picture of sexuality, a picture that remained unstaged. As for Hamlet, he was 'a youth deeply involved in politics, rid of illusions, sarcastic, passionate and brutal; a young rebel who has about him something of the charm of James Dean.' The tragedy, like a sponge, 'immediately absorbed all the problems of our time'. There were scholars, for one Professor Helen Gardner, at Oxford, who regarded Kott as arrogant; others were ready to accept his obsession with power politics. At Stratford Peter Hall said that for the decade of the 1960s the play would be about disillusionment which produced an apathy so deep that 'commitment to politics, to religion, or to life' was impossible. Though this was the right news for young people now prepared fanatically to look back in anger, it was an uninspiring invitation to *Hamlet*. I tried, without noticeable pleasure, to think of Horatio looking down on his dead friend and saying elegiacally: 'Good night, sweet prince, and flights of angels sing thee to thy rest from the problems of commitment to life and politics.'

II

Anyway, here he was: a disillusioned Prince betrayed by the older generation, in apathetic rebellion against the Establishment (never the easiest word to define, but for years an amorphous dragon). Warner was tall, angular, and frail, yet until near the end he seemed to be a small Hamlet and quite unprincely, not that this was a quality for the 'prison' of his Elsinore: there was nothing to speak for the Hamlet Ophelia had known. He was anti-romantic, gauche, brusque and nasal, not always audible. When his 'antic disposition' was on he began by wearing spectacles and a funny hat. He lay around on the floor. At length, with his lank blond hair ruffled, his cloak rucked up like a belted mackintosh, with a rust-red muffler about his neck, it was the picture of a rather scruffy, inconspicuous undergraduate from a minor Wittenberg debating society, or a worried youth leaving a bar in the King's Road late for an engagement. This was plainly the approved contemporary image, the Hamlet of the 1960s: if there was one person he did not resemble, it was the heir to Denmark, 'the glass of fashion and the mould of form'. Quite, quite down, could he ever have been up? Nobody would have dreamt of summoning C. E. Montague from sixty years earlier: 'All over faults, but a regular globe of passion and romance, with huge subterranean caverns and flames of fire in it.' A natural resident of his Elsinore, Warner did show us round, gloomily omitting nothing, as if to say: 'You see, this is what we have to put up with.' It was apparent that he pleased people of his own generation immensely. Anyone's first Hamlet must be the centrepiece in his gallery of royal Elsinore, and I suspected that for many at Stratford this Hamlet, with whom they could identify, was their first. The première ended among storming cheers. That night, and thereafter, crowds at the stage door might have been waiting to salute a pop star. Through the season, on *Hamlet* nights, partisan queues beleaguered the theatre. It was an hour for rebellion, and Warner grew into the centre of a cult, saying in the words of Shakespeare – and probably with distant applause from Jan Kott – all that his admirers wanted him to say.

Though seniors could hesitate, they acknowledged the actor's understanding of his task. His grief was not imposed. A soul adrift, 'I do not know why yet I live to say "This thing's to do"', spoken slowly with arms outflung, was the obvious epigraph for the performance. Warner became likelier towards the close, from the churchyard (where the Gravedigger would have held the floor at Elsinore's TUC) to his bantering of a disapproving, officious Osric and the last passage after a ferocious duel. There Hamlet thrust the cup upon the King, stood watching the death-throes, and moved back with a dazed smile of triumph, relief that it was over at last, that action had been forced upon him. The look of triumph lingered as he sank upon a bench, kissed his father's miniature and himself sank into death; nothing became him like his end.

Yet, watching the baffled youth in his Doubting Castle of despair, my occasional admiration had seldom warmed into the finer excitement. Where was the genuine feeling between Hamlet and Horatio? The homage before the Play scene became perfunctory. Then, too, Hamlet could shy off, embarrassed, from the need to express himself poetically. Arguing away very, very slowly, he would suddenly 'start like a guilty thing upon a fearful summons' when a speech insisted on making its own music – and in Shakespeare, to the alarm of several young players of the sixties, a speech can insist. Some of us wondered, at the première, whether verse-into-prose could be an answer to an austere examiner. Young listeners had no worry whatever. They were hearing these statements for a first time and they could sympathise, in terms of their own day, with a man who had been through it all. The fact that glory could wane to a weary naturalism was wholly unimportant, except to elders who wanted more than glum exposition and a gaucherie that at times was engaging, at others not: these were demanding enough to ask for a stronger sense of language and to be stirred to the quick, and the 1965-model Hamlet would leave it late.

III

He had started badly: no terror in the scene with the Ghost, though probably it was unfair to ask him to act with his father as represented here. King Hamlet (another improbable device) arrived as an immense puppet-apparition, far larger than life, about ten feet high with a huge artificial head, a Colossus in armour towering above young Hamlet crouched between his arms; from within the figure Patrick Magee's voice emerged sonorously. Doubtless finding it hard to recover, Warner was only moderate in the first scene, greyly, meagrely spoken, with Rosencrantz and Guildenstern. Competent with the Players, he proved to be unexpectedly out of tune during the Closet scene – another entry for the Ghost – where Elizabeth Spriggs's Gertrude would be among the best in living memory, a shallow woman terrified by the pressure of events she could not comprehend. Claudius (Brewster Mason), dominating, corrupt usurper, did not remind me in the least of my first King who had a habit of sprawling round Elsinore, wearing a crown. (In London that winter Mason, appropriately masked, also played the Ghost, reconsidered for the better.)

Polonius (Tony Church) was the man for his King, a personage shifty and sententious, if fussily irritated at home when, losing his thread, he had no notion what 'closes in the consequence' could have meant. Until her father's death, Ophelia (Glenda Jackson) had a mind of her own that also delighted the rebellious. If never a wilting blossom, in danger of prettification, she had not prepared us for that rapped-out retort, 'My lord, I do not know', when Polonius asked her about Hamlet's tenders of affection. In her madness, entering, according to the First Quarto direction, 'playing on a lute and her hair downe, singing', she could still be recognised as the girl of the earlier scenes, no young actress letting herself go at random. Janet Suzman, who succeeded her in London, was perhaps, though not much, gentler.

John Bury had designed a gleaming, shining coal set that gave an impression of ebony and black marble – actually it was formica – with hints of silver. At the back were two immense doors and on either side of the main set inner rooms decorated with fading tapestries. For the opening scene a great cannon and the sound of strained voices that talked for talking's sake were enough to bring us to the midnight platform. Directing with unusually unobtrusive craft in a text based upon the Second Quarto, and with such a delighted theatrical effect as the chase in the dark after the Closet scene, Peter Hall began the night with an act that lasted unbroken for two and a half hours, excellent discipline for any audience. Nobody protested at Stratford.

In years ahead such a Hamlet as this, the soul of

disillusion, would cease to be modish. The experiment had
to be tried; but we, too, were progressively disillusioned as
a magnificent part shrank to the proportions of the mid-
sixties, and while the lines failed to ring.

IV

Just previously I had gone to Bristol Old Vic to see (and
undeniably to hear) a much more satisfying Hamlet,
though without any loaded appeal to one generation. It is
usually evident after twenty minutes or so whether the
Prince will dwell with us as a truthful portrait, one face of
many, or whether he can live only on the tightrope of a
director's caprice. Richard Pasco had never known a
tightrope, though at rehearsal a single scene could have
troubled him.

Merely to sit among the centuries at Bristol Theatre
Royal means a lot. Pleasure was doubled at a *Hamlet* where
Pasco, naturally an intellectual and as affecting a speaker as
any on our stage, offered what until then must have been
the performance of his career. Always he had thought
himself into Shakespearian verse instead of skimming it
with misplaced optimism. Like many people's, my Hamlet
had been (and is) composite, and on his Bristol showing
Pasco would be prominent in any final mosaic: possibly for
the prose scene, so gently phrased in its grace and honesty,
with Horatio before the Play; the verbal sparring with the
King after Polonius's death; and the courtly salute to
Laertes, 'Give me your pardon, sir', before the duel that
must end all. When this Hamlet died the man of Ophelia's
panegyric had died with him.

It was in the Ghost scene that Pasco had to fight, ever an
actor's headache and made harder at Brisol by the decision
of Alvin Rakoff, who directed, to keep the Ghost invisible.
We heard a rushing wind over the battlements and what

sounded like painful effort, a labouring heart-beat that reminded me of *Kubla Khan*, 'As if this earth in fast thick pants were breathing'. But there was neither presence nor, remotely, voice. Hamlet had to paraphrase certain lines, as if he were repeating a message on a supernatural telephone, thus, ' 'Tis given out that, sleeping in thy orchard, a serpent stung thee'; and it was Hamlet himself that cried, 'O horrible! O, horrible! most horrible!' Richard Pasco managed it, but I did not think he should have been required to do so. Often, what a director pictures with the text on his lap can be theatrically a blunder: as the O'Casey character says, 'I see no magnificent meanin' jumpin' out of that'.

Rakoff, indeed, could obtrude. He cut the First Player's speech; and he split 'O, what a rogue and peasant slave' – this was more workable – so that Hamlet thought aloud the first part while gazing at the Players and resumed at 'Am I a coward?' when they had left the stage with Polonius. The director had no room for the comic preliminaries to the Graveyard scene. We were aware throughout of a clipped text and yet the revival could develop excitingly, with such performances as Barbara Leigh-Hunt's sad, bewildered Ophelia and her heart-rending courtesies in the Mad scene; as Polonius (Frank Middlemass) who indicated his affection for Laertes as much as any I had known; and Osric (Gawn Grainger), a devil of a fellow about the Court, no popinjay as he used always to be played though, ironically, Hamlet's longest speech about him ('and many more of the same bevy, that I know the drossy age dotes on') was seldom heard. At Bristol it was, as it had to be, Hamlet's night: a loving soul driven to a desperate act, and in regicide stabbing the King with all the force of his long-pent rage, such avenging violence as we had seldom met (we could cast back to 'For though I am not splenitive and rash, yet have I in me something dangerous'). On the return that night I was envying anybody who had just seen the play afresh through Pasco's eyes, and who had heard it through his voice.

Pasco, now forty, appeared again, about eighteen months later, at the head of a Bristol company that was going to North America in the ensuing spring (of 1967). This time he had not to paraphrase the Ghost. After a quick shock and acceptance I forgot Val May's choice of Regency costume. It suited Pasco: no irrelevant impressions distracted me even if, here and there, a pose had to be reminiscent of some early nineteenth-century romantic engraving, a passage from a world of period melancholy. Never an extrovert, he phrased from the heart of the speeches with a music controlled and varied, and (not every actor does it) he obeyed his own advice to the Players. Passion flashed when, during 'O, what a rogue and peasant slave!' he sent the throne hurtling down the steps; later, in the Closet scene's rising anger; and at the end, every challenge taken, when he moved (as he had done before) to a furious avenger. Above all, North America would find a spoken Hamlet: Pasco was not a man for back-room mumbling or for jagged, saw-toothed Shakespeare, like another poet's 'juts of pointed rock': scorning to wrench and falsify a line, he acted with a unity that defied the pedantically exigent. Barbara Leigh-Hunt presented again the fearful honesty of Ophelia's dementia. Horatio (Frank Barrie) was loyalty personified, a man for any confidence, though curiously Hamlet does not tell his 'fellow-student' all. Directors have struggled with Horatio, who is forever wandering about the Court, presumably on long leave from Wittenberg (he came to Elsinore to see King Hamlet's funeral). It may appear odd that the part, fourth in order, is as long as it is (265 lines); still, in the cut text, he has to lose more than forty of his lines, those when, to fill up time, he talks of 'this post-haste and romage in the land'. The Ghost is likely to appear at any moment and no one can concentrate.

Though for years we have assumed that the philosopher-student from Hamlet's Wittenberg (it was Luther's university) is of Hamlet's own age, it is not improbable now that he will be presented as a mature don; in a National production by Peter Hall he was spectacled, bearded and a trifle shabby; nothing like the 'Charles, his friend', honest-youth figure of tradition. We have also, and tiresomely, known him to be acted as a 'hearty', his demeanour wildly at odds with the lines. Tom Stoppard might find a hint for another play in a look at Hamlet's Wittenberg experience.

v

About now I spent eighty minutes (the full running time) at a chaotic mish-mash, described untruthfully as *Hamlet*, at one of the very minor London fringe theatres. Gratefully, I remember nothing at all except the absence of Rosencrantz and Guildenstern, that exasperatingly inseparable pair of shadows involved briefly in espionage and surveillance. In his film Olivier, too, cut them altogether. They ought to be essential to the plot, but no one seems to worry much if their share is unresolved.

For a decade or so, during my early *Hamlets*, I would watch competent young actors – one no doubt doubling Rosencrantz (or Guildenstern) with Osric – trying manfully to suggest that there was more difference between them than between Tweedledum and Tweedledee. The grandly sonorous names, known among important Danish families, occur apparently in Wittenberg student records about 1590; they suited Shakespeare's purpose as young men, much of an age, who were prepared to spy on Hamlet for the King's benefit and in hope of favours to come. They are disgraceful time-servers – just how disgraceful we know from Hamlet's speech to them before the Players arrive: 'My uncle is King of Denmark, and those who would make mows at him while my father lived give twenty, forty, fifty, a hundred ducats apiece for his picture in little.' (In a North American modern-dress production which Gielgud directed for Richard Burton, the point was clarified when Hamlet glanced at the small portrait of Claudius that Rosencrantz wore on his necktie.)

These are the alleged friends of Hamlet of whom Claudius speaks as 'being of young days brought up with him / And since so neighboured to his youth and haviour', and to whom Gertrude says flatteringly: 'Sure I am two men there are not living / To whom he more adheres.' They go off, fawning, to their task where Hamlet at first greets them cordially in the old Wittenberg manner: 'My excellent good friends. How dost thou, Guildenstern? Ah, Rosencrantz! Good lads, how do ye both?' But he guesses why they are there and urges them to admit it 'by the consonancy of your youth, by the obligation of our ever preservèd love'. They have to confess the King had sent for them; thenceforward they are of the enemy. Hamlet makes it clear to Guildenstern in the Recorder scene: 'Do you think I am easier to be played on than a pipe? Call me what instrument you will, you can fret me, yet you cannot play upon me.'

Before the Closet scene Claudius tells them of their coming journey to England with Hamlet, and they are ready with the right replies, Rosencrantz especially portentous in a speech familiar only in the 'eternity' version:

> The cease of majesty
> Dies not alone; but like a gulf doth draw
> What's near it with it. 'Tis a massy wheel
> Fixed on the summit of the highest mount,
> To whose huge spokes ten thousand lesser things

Are mortis'd and adjoin'd; which when it falls,
Each small annexment, petty consequence,
Attends the boist'rous ruin. Never alone
Did the king sigh, but with a general groan.

(My first full-version Rosencrantz had some laborious
moments in trying to present the huge spokes and the
massy wheel.) After the Closet scene the pair pursue
Hamlet to take him to the King: a lively passage for a
director. The last we see of them – Rosencrantz here is the
only speaker – is on the journey across the plain after
Fortinbras and the Norwegian captain have passed, and
before Hamlet's soliloquy, 'How all occasions'. We are to
hear in Hamlet's letter to Horatio of the grapple with the
pirate ship, and a single phrase: 'Rosencrantz and Guildenstern hold their course for England; of them I have much to
tell thee.' True, though generally it is only in the full text
that we learn of Hamlet's stratagem and of the two men
moving on, unknowing, to England and their deaths
('Rosencrantz and Guildenstern are dead' says the First
English Ambassador if he is there to say it).

That is all we hear of the pair, once known in theatre
slang as 'the knife and the fork' because they 'feed' Hamlet.
Richard Burton said when he played Hamlet in New York
during 1964: 'I can only think they were very nodding
acquaintances, Rosencrantz and Guildenstern doing most
of the nodding.' And Gielgud: 'On doesn't quite see those
two, with Horatio and Hamlet, having a midnight binge.
They're horrid creatures, really – just toadies to the King.
All the people round Hamlet are very second-rate, and
Hamlet loathes second-rate things.' As personages they
never escape from each other. There is a tale of Robert
Atkins coming from a long casting session and rumbling to
his neighbour: 'Don't know their Shakespeare. I said to this
fellow, "Will you give me your Rosencrantz, old son?"

And, can you credit it, he gave me his Guildenstern.'
Whatever their function in the narrative, the fellow-
students come to us as spare parts. Professor Arthur Colby
Sprague, when he wrote on doubling, cited a pleasantly
implausible playbill from Sheffield in 1843 when Hamlet
was 'supported' by Mr East as Rosencrantz, Mr West as
Francisco, and Mr South as the Priest. Possibly Guildenstern was a Mr North?

The pair so delighted the dramatist, Tom Stoppard, that
he put them at the centre of one of his early plays,
Rosencrantz and Guildenstern are Dead. When I met this, done
by amateurs at the Edinburgh Festival in 1966, I said
something to the effect that it was as lucid as a mist rolling
up across East Lothian from the Firth of Forth. Nor was I
much impressed by a National production in the following
year, with actors as engaging as John Stride and Edward
Petherbridge. I was wrong: it seems to me now that the
play has a witty theatrical edge. Stoppard wrote of the
attendant lords who are brought from darkness, and into
darkness go: 'They are told very little of what is going on,
and much of what they are told isn't true. So I see them
much more clearly as a couple of bewildered innocents
rather than as a couple of henchmen.' One of them
observes: 'I feel like a spectator – an appalling business. The
only thing that makes it bearable is the irrational belief that
somebody interesting will come on in a moment.' The
people that do arrive, in an intermittent onrush of familiar
characters, are the people of *Hamlet*. We are left with a pair
of principals whose very names are interchangeable and
who spend their time trying hazily to fill the gaps until
another perplexing swoop through the corridors of
Elsinore. It is easy (as I found at first) to let the text slide
away as a dramatist's indulgence, but one does become
haunted by the blank predicament of the pair and by such
lines as the description of England as 'a conspiracy of

cartographers'. The piece does not always grip the attention, but, as somebody put it, we never know where the dialogue, which has the irregular bounce of a Rugby football, will swerve next. Perhaps we can call it an exercise in shadow choreography.

VI

Rosencrantz and Guildenstern – and how much better they sound than the First Quarto's Rosencraft and Gilderstone! – were present and, if I recall, moderately correct in an Edinburgh Festival production during August 1968. Edinburgh even then was not fully set into the type of Festival city that it is now. In *As You Like It*, asked where she dwells, Rosalind, in the guise of a young man (Ganymede), uses a thoughtless analogy: 'Here in the skirts of the forest, like fringe upon a petticoat.' In the Edinburgh of 1987 there is infinitely more of the fringe than the petticoat. By 1968 this was advancing: you could hardly walk down any reasonably accessible street without discovering some temporary theatre, part of a patchwork where, for a brief season, you might see practically anything between Aeschylus or a young man's epic in garret or cellar. The wider view, the historical-theatrical, was changeless, yet still surprising, however superficially acquainted you were with it: the Castle ruling all, the serrated ridge of the Old Town where the Middle Ages run down towards Holyrood; the lion of Arthur's Seat, the hidden Dean Village, yonder those towering 'lands', elsewhere the classical crescents and squares, or the sudden perpetual amazement that is Ann Street. With Wendy I stayed near here when, after Eric Keown's death and with Ronald Searle working in France, we no longer travelled back at night to the immense silence of Dirleton. At Festival time the centre of the city's stage, no mere tassel of its fringe, continued to be the Assembly Hall of the Church of Scotland where Guthrie, one drenched evening in 1947, discerned a theatre; John Knox's guardian statue had never been animated in distaste.

At the Assembly Hall in 1968, Tom Courtenay, aged thirty-one, a lovable player prepared for most matters, appeared as another student Prince, neither lank nor scarf-throttled and far less debatable than at Stratford. In a production by Caspar Wrede, Courtenay appeared to have deliberately subdued himself. Not a naturally compelling speaker – he had never been primarily a classical man – his swift, crackling, frequently colloquial delivery could not bear comparison with Shakespearians who 'signed with conflagration the empty moors of air'. Yet, on the night, we soon ceased to listen to him phrase by phrase; rather, we took the sense of a passage, the mood of a sequence, and became closely involved once more in the narrative of *Hamlet*. Doubtless Shakespeare would have wished this, though I assume he would have liked more vocal virtuosity, more evidence of interpretation, a princelier demeanour. Still, the performance was logical, honest, touching, and never caught up in the need for point making that so troubled William Charles Macready. The production had similar merits: certainly none of that 'masking' perilous on the Assembly Hall platform where actors, no more than anywhere else, are seldom transparent when standing in front of a colleague; and an avoidance of tricky entrances and exits through the audience that had so annoyed Eric Keown and Ivor Brown. It was a pleasure to have a production faithful to a text not uncomfortably cut. No room, in general, for irrelevant complaint in the tones of a woman, bent upon criticism at all costs, who at a comedy revival denounced the door knobs. Dilys Hamlett's Queen (the King was commonplace) took a realistic view, never trying to force the part out of proportion; and Edgar

Wreford haunted Elsinore with a Ghost who this time had
the face of a skull.

VII

Wreford had been a Birmingham Repertory player, one of
'Jackson's lot'. It was in Birmingham (1969) that I met the
next Hamlet: an actor who reached the front pages before a
word was spoken, simply because Richard Chamberlain,
an American, had been popular in the television part of Dr
Kildare. Suffering from acute single-mindedness, I had not
seen the programme, something that at any rate stopped me
from being dazzled by fame that had flared in another
medium. When the play was over, in a production by Peter
Dews, one might have said (and not condescendingly) as
Ellen Terry to Benson after his Lyceum début as Paris:
'Well done for first done.' This Hamlet, personable and in
his late twenties, was essentially generous and free from all
contriving: no fresh light on the man, but scarcely anything
except an over-calculated death scene that sounded false. If
the sorrow did not strike deeply, it was there. Chamberlain
expressed each scene as he reached it, without prefatory
fussing. We did not leave the theatre recalling a lost neurotic
or an alabaster profile. This was just an intelligent young
man whose theatrical skill we accepted without feeling
necessarily that it added to the sum of our memories. Major
performances were, and are, so rare that we could respect a
Hamlet who took a sound second class degree. He was a
good actor, and that is still an honourable epithet when
superlatives are blown about like sequins.

On the whole, I did not regret the decision by Peter Dews
to provide a 'late Tsarist' setting, a decadent northern Court
from the early years of the century: Finlay James set it in an
art nouveau frame of wrought ironwork (dull gold under the
lights), elaborately staircased. One or two ideas I hoped,

but vainly, might grow into later revivals: before the first curtain-fall, while the King, above, spoke of madness, Ophelia (Gemma Jones), after her repulse by Hamlet, was kneeling distraught below. As real a performance as any was Brian Oulton's wiseacre-Polonius who uttered the Precepts as if they had occurred to him that morning. Oddly, in these surroundings, the King reminded me of a regal Volpone; but he and his wife, who could have been a contralto hostess from an Edwardian memoir, and kept her two husbands' photographs on the dressing table, did preserve the spirit of the night.

Chamberlain, I thought, was a more plausible Hamlet than the Scots actor, Nicol Williamson, who about the same time was playing in London at the Round House (a former engine shed in Chalk Farm, vast and a shade puzzling until one discovered the way around). The revival excited younger people as much as Warner's had at Stratford yet this Hamlet would have been anxiously observed in Elsinore only because he was a dangerous person who never sought any reputation as a courtier and a scholar, and from whom it would be wise to stand apart. Aged thirty then, and celebrated for his work in John Osborne's *Inadmissible Evidence*, Williamson was a tall, authoritative actor, like others of this time sharply influenced by the needs of modern drama. Theirs was a world of the vernacular, an egalitarian place in which princeliness was ignored and talk of the traditional Hamlet had simply to be brushed away. Where a comparably dominating actor, Wolfit, used to wear the language as a ceremonial robe that frayed at length when his voice was over-worked, Williamson's robe had always to be a thing of shreds and patches. Like Pooh-Bah, his Hamlet was born sneering; excessively ill-tempered, it prickled with awkward vowel sounds. At the Round House I listened for an inspired revelation that never came; never the sensation in the midriff that some of us have when looking down from a great height.

Probably approval of the reading, and it was strongly approved, was a final reaction from a period long before it. It could recall a conventional Hamlet who spent his night paying out the lines as if they were woods curving smoothly across a bowling green on a June afternoon, one delivery like the next. That could wane to mellifluous monotony. A preferred form in the mid- and late 1960s could be equally monotonous, but from a region where any beauty of tone was an anachronism. One argument ran that, if a speech sounded well, the actor could not appreciate what he was saying. I thought we had almost got over this; but a young critic in 1987 was praising a director's 'essential argument that the staging of a Shakespeare play must cut through the fustian of history and classical tradition; the convention which presents Shakespeare's work as blood-less poetic rhetoric, spoken by sweet-voiced actors in gorgeous pantomime apparel, is merely a convention adhered to out of long custom'. (I wonder how this will sound in 1999?)

Twenty years ago such a performance as Williamson's splenitive Hamlet, speaking with the voice of the time, was eminently fashionable. It was at the centre of a production by Tony Richardson that swept the play back and forth across the two levels of a wide, bare thrust stage: good if the tragedy had not been simplified to a plain revenge drama, with a Hamlet who would gladly have killed Claudius at any time in a fit of anger and finished off the night then and there. I remember the treatment of the Ghost, heard but not seen: all we knew of it was a tortured, echoing voice that swooped through the building while Hamlet, listening to it, was pinned between converging spotlights. At the end of the Play scene, instead of accustomed tumult and clatter, the King and Hamlet stared for a moment at each other before Hamlet's cry, 'What, frighted with false fire!' Other players I found less contentious than their Prince: the Welsh Claudius of Anthony Hopkins, Gordon Jackson's Scottish Horatio, a forlorn Ophelia (Marianne Faithful). The short version included Reynaldo but no Second Gravedigger – bad news for Yaughan – and no Fortinbras: a difficulty, perhaps, with 'He was likely, had he been put on, to have proved most royal.'

14
ROYAL ASSEMBLY: 1969–75

I

GRADUALLY, as we entered the 1970s, experiment (or rebellion) in the grand national game of Shakespeare slackened a little, as it was doing in matters outside the theatre. It was seven years since Peter Hall – later followed at Stratford by another Cambridge man, the twenty-eight-year-old Trevor Nunn – had said that 'the whole thing, stage, setting, costumes, speaking, creative acting', had to be in a world of experiment. Peter Brook provided the first and practically the last memorable director's coup of the new decade with his *Midsummer Night's Dream* circus-fashion, that even the orthodox had to cheer. It was now that *Hamlet*s came together in a royal assembly, none arrogantly defiant, though I am sure that Ben Greet certainly, and Robert Atkins possibly, as guardians of tradition in their day, might still have protested across the years.

During the spring of 1970 the first production was a replay by Peter Dews of his 1969 'Tsarist' revival, again at Birmingham Repertory but with a new and older Prince; Alec McCowen, at forty-four, had succeeded Richard Chamberlain. It was agreeable, after the publicised Round House revival, not to ask why a Hamlet must be so unsympathetic, 'teasy' they would have said at The Lizard. McCowen (who had carried the night in a dramatisation of

Hadrian the Seventh) was a mercurial actor with a mildly gritty manner that worried no one. At Birmingham we could accept him as a Hamlet who could just have missed a First at Wittenberg, never frittering away the months in some remote undergraduate project. Boyishly slight, quick in mind, he was wiser than many players who had had wisdom thrust upon them, but like several Hamlets of the day he wanted royalty of voice, the invaluable gift of sound. He was a more complex figure than his charming predecessor. Where Chamberlain had offered an acceptable popular idea without taking it much further, McCowen was more taxing, though in his distillation of meaning from phrase or speech, he was proficient enough not to let the footnotes and appendices show. We observed his restraint on the battlements after the Ghost had melted into the morning air; his frown at the First Player's 'Pyrrhus stood / And like a neutral to his will and matter, / *Did nothing*'; his advice to the Players, tactful in tone and temper; and, in 'How all occasions', the near-scream at 'Let all sleep'. Not a night of point-making, it was a production from the same mood as Dews's earlier one and in the same setting, both decorative and complying with the demands of the Elizabethan stage. There was so important a return from the former cast as Brian Oulton's Polonius, sententious man of affairs, his standing at Elsinore never in dispute.

From Hamlets that now came upon each other quickly, the first (1970) would be Alan Howard, in his fifth year at Stratford and, among contemporary actors, the likeliest heir to the Danish throne; he was then thirty-two. His youthful melancholy was more settled than that of many Hamlets. The Ghost's revelation overthrew a noble mind; he might speak of an 'antic disposition', but it had gone deeper when he faced Ophelia. Trevor Nunn, who directed, had established this scene in the castle chapel, the King and Polonius hidden in confessional boxes; Hamlet had no cause to be aware of their presence, and indeed he was not. He spoke 'To be, or not to be' while kneeling at the altar. During the colloquy with Ophelia, 'It hath made me mad' came urgently from a Hamlet of 'sweet bells jangled, out of tune and harsh'; Claudius, when the scene ended, knew that madness in great ones must not unwatched go. The Prince appeared to us to be a manic depressive, and it made sense in the context of the production. Howard could speak his calmer ratiocinative passages with unmauled truth.

Denmark, from the opening midnight chill, was a realm of evil dreams, something stressed in productions of the time. We realised the domestic strain from the moment when the King, brutal sensualist with a politician's brain, barked out his formal phrases among the white-furred puppets of his Court: the Prince, conspicuous in his 'inky cloak', was the one black-clad figure, as he would be through much of the night. He did not compromise: Ophelia and the Queen were in danger, and his attack on Polonius was the fiercest in recollection; when at last he had been secured, the King, overwhelmed, repaid him by furious punches. The tragedy became more surely a document in madness after Ophelia had been driven into desperate terms, an agonised sight of the abyss. If it was not my favourite *Hamlet*, I recognised the consistency and impact of the production on an uncluttered stage; the leap of the imagination with which Alan Howard responded, and his quiet intensity at the end; David Waller's 'bloat King' who, after Hamlet had stabbed him, took the poison voluntarily; Brenda Bruce as Gertrude, passing from infatuated submission to her grief, expressed without a single movement, in the narration of Ophelia's death; Helen Mirren as the broken girl, and Sebastian Shaw as a Polonius of immense complacency, pomp and circumstance.

Jonathan Miller's fame as a classical director was growing. When, in the autumn of 1970, he did *Hamlet* for the
Oxford and Cambridge Shakespeare Company, a union of
the best talent from both universities, he cut the first scene
and took us straight to Court: for me a gentle shock
because, writing a programme note (at a distance from the
Arts Theatre, Cambridge) I had suggested that Barnardo's
'Who's there?', at the outset of the midnight vigil, was the
most exciting speech in all drama. Later, other directors
would choose this inexplicable cut – hearing of it, a
Budapest professor put his head between his hands before
addressing me in musical, if incomprehensible, Magyar –
but Miller, I believe, was the first to startle us in his new
consideration of Elsinore. It was as astringent as original.
Hamlet arrived immediately at curtain-rise, taking a
position in a corner of the Court while other entrants stared
at him in distaste. How would the Prince behave now?
Probably in one of his erratic moods? There he stood while
Claudius, an unsmiling, crop-haired martinet, read from an
official manuscript much of his opening speech ('Though
yet of Hamlet, our dear brother's death, the memory be
green'). Upon the battlements, our only visit to them, the
Ghost, instead of orating in sepulchral grandeur, a clanking
envoy from the eternal fires, sat by his son and talked to him
in the manner of a soul inexpressibly fatigued and hopeless
(another for the convocation of phantoms). Hamlet, we
found, was a brooding adolescent, incalculable, neurotic
and not at all likeable. When he said 'I am alone' we felt that
this was what he had to be: the world delighted him not and
it must have disturbed those round him to be regarded,
more or less, as a foul and pestilent congregation of
vapours. Recluse that he was, he must goad himself
forward. Hugh Thomas, in no sense a romantic, Ophelia's
ideal, was a bitterly baffled student. Though Elsinore
believed him to be a danger, he was not dangerous enough

until the last, after the duel in which he moved from petulant confidence to furious rage, he made us aware that Denmark would have had a king indeed. But now it was at the very frontier of the undiscovered country, and the rest was silence. He went off-stage to die, something that would have sent into a decline such an actor as Beerbohm Tree who provided a heavenly choir to fortify his last centre-stage minutes.

Collectors of variation would have had a fruitful night at Cambridge: Miller, as in most of his work, examined the play as if he had picked up the book oblivious of the pressure of tradition. I could not recall a revival in which the Ghost, back in the Closet scene, had embraced his former wife. Other things were less alarming: for example, the surly King, disdaining a formal prayer, argued out his conscience in the presence of Osric, a man, devious to the end, who would be ready as a courtier to Fortinbras, the new power, patron of the future. Ophelia's mad scenes rose consistently from the character of a sulky, self-willed, infatuated girl. At the end the King faced death almost as the climax of a ritual. One actor contrived ingeniously to treble the Ghost, the Player King, and Fortinbras.

Though I cannot conceive yet why Miller jettisoned the first scene (he did not bother about a programme note), the production had a director's flourish, by which I still mean a potent use of the theatre theatrical. Even if brought up on H. W. Fowler (who, long ago, had been Le Mesurier's inspiration), I never agreed with his gentle ghost when he defined 'flourish' simply as a rhetorical embellishment or – charmingly – 'ostentatious waving of weapon, hand, etc.'

II

Early in 1971 another director, Anthony Page, at the Cambridge Theatre in London, agreed with Miller by removing the first scene, a perilous gash, a very limb lopp'd off. Alan Bates, to my regret, was visible before a word was spoken, entering in customary solemn black before the court had assembled. Again we had lost a passage once deemed to be inviolable. Elsewhere during the night I had not noticed cutting more obtrusive: not so much the removal of the Gravedigger's early verbiage, but an intermittent mincing of the text: the loss, say, of Polonius's introduction of the Players and Hamlet's 'A station like the herald Mercury'.

Décor was unexpected, a metal-box Elsinore. It was nearly forty years since Theodore Komisarjevsky's so-called 'aluminium' *Macbeth* at Stratford. Now at the Cambridge we had, in effect, an aluminium *Hamlet*, set in sliding panels that, as they flicked to and fro, caused me to think less of 'Denmark's a prison', which could have been the intention, than to wonder whether Hamlet might not be missing some Danish tube train. Alan Bates, who inhabited these bare, gleaming spaces, a relaxed, cogently spoken actor, aged thirty-six, was not generally a Shakespearian, though he had played Richard III at Stratford, Ontario; brought up with the Royal Court company in its explosive period, he was in the original cast of *Look Back in Anger*. In this *Hamlet* he missed few points without making me profoundly aware of any: no doubt he could have graced the Danish throne, yet he had little magnetism, no touch of splendour in a correct, rather dispiriting performance that down the years has slipped into the ruck. Round him the standard was respectable: a moderate Polonius and Ophelia; some dubious casting (a tough, compact Fortin-bras, not much like the 'delicate and tender prince'). Most performances, as I think Desmond MacCarthy said, can leave traces on the sand when the tide has ebbed; this one had in Douglas Wilmer a smooth compact usurper, and in Celia Johnson's Gertrude, with a voice like brittle spun glass, the portrait of a puzzled mind, regally tactful in small things but foolishly overcome.

We had to suppose in August 1972 that strangers to London might have held, wrongly, that Shakespeare was a normal part of a West End programme. This was because another *Hamlet* had arrived, again at the Cambridge Theatre in Seven Dials, and with a principal, Ian McKellen, who in a short time had grown highly reputed; mainly because of his bold attack, his unconcealed pleasure in language and the response to suffering with which he had acted both Richard II and Marlowe's Edward II for the travelling Prospect company as well as upon a London stage. It was a little too soon for some hyperbole which, within a decade, he justified; but this Hamlet, at thirty-two, had an emotional certainty and a naturalism which once or twice could go too far (as in 'You shouldn't have believed me' to Ophelia). Such details as a quiver in the voice were undistracting. His passion had a ring. Without seeking major epithets too soon, I applauded McKellen during the Play scene particularly; before this he followed William Charles Macready's habit of striding from side to side of the stage, twirling his handkerchief above his head. At Edinburgh one night in 1846, when Macready did this at the line, 'I must be idle', he was hissed from the audience by his envious American rival, Edwin Forrest, who claimed afterwards that he was right to object to a *pas de mouchoir*.

In McKellen's first scene with the Players, 'O, what a rogue and peasant slave', was in the acted text immediately after the Hecuba speech, had a splendid sustained fury and ultimate decision. What did trouble me was some of the minor editing, designed presumably for a lazy listener. If not, why did we get such a line as 'When Fortinbras of Norway did him slay', or hear 'My nephew Hamlet, and my son' in the King's first speech, and after the Play Hamlet's 'For thou dost know, O Damon dear, *the world has fallen apart*'? During the duel the King insisted that he would throw a 'pearl' into the cup (not 'in the cup an union shall he throw'). Editors who tinker in this way forget that few listeners to Shakespeare pause to debate the meaning or shape or syntax of a phrase already gone.

Robert Chetwyn, who directed, conveyed the midnight chill, but though generally the employment of a mirrored stage could impress, one had to be wary when the recorded voice of 'thy father's spirit' rose from the midst of a multiplicity of reflected ghosts. Undoubtedly a device which did not help Hamlet at all was his confinement in a strait-jacket at 'How all occasions'. Once, I understand, a modern director, doubtless looking forward to 'Denmark's a prison' (II.2), a phrase much quoted, made Hamlet act his early scenes wearing manacles. (Ernest Milton's anger, had he known this, would have been worth recording.) John Woodvine, at the Cambridge, was a harsh Claudius, not a man to bother about the secondary suavities. It was all the more valid for Faith Brook to play the Queen as a fuddled doll.

III

Though the actual site of Shakespeare's Globe is hidden somewhere beneath a brewery on Bankside, any effort to open a theatre not far from it, among that dark battalion of warehouses, those sinister brick canyons – Ivor Brown's favourite walk – is bound to get a certain sympathy: this, it is true, may falter during the effort of reaching the place; but we can think of the history of the Globe to cheer us. Aligned (so a scholar has said) more or less accurately to the midsummer sunrise, it was the most easterly of the Southwark theatres. The wooden Theatre – no other name – which finally supplied the main fabric of the Globe had been the first purpose-built playhouse, raised in Shoreditch during 1576 by James Burbage, father of the great actor Richard, and himself a joiner-turned-actor. When its lease expired more than two decades later, not long after James's death, the Burbage sons were in dispute with the owner of the site. Transiently, the small Curtain quite close – it could have been the 'wooden O' of the *Henry V* Chorus – made a home for the Lord Chamberlain's Men with whom Shakespeare served as dramatist and, we gather, usually reliable actor.

At length, after useless parleying and at the end of December 1598, the Burbages took their own way. Under darkness and ignoring every effort to stop them, they and their helpers dismantled the materials of the Theatre and transferred them over the river to Bankside; it has been suggested that the timbers might have been slid across the frozen Thames on a bleak night of the bleak winter. Anyway, they would create the polygonal structure of the Globe, and there the Lord Chamberlain's Men (who one day would be the King's Men) began a new life, Richard Burbage leading the company.

True, the Bankside Globe Playhouse (a nicely ambiguous name), which had a season in 1972, turned out to be one of the draughtier semi-tents that in practice could have inspired few romantic imaginings: plenty of room but everything all too temporary: on the first *Hamlet* night the air bit shrewdly, it was very cold. Burbage might have accepted the general shape of the stage, and the almost unvaried light would have been natural to him. Other matters he might have argued about: the presentation of Denmark as some repressive military dictatorship, and much agile scrambling round ladders and balcony.

Peter Coe, the director, had been consistent with his police-state background, the period's popular 'Denmark's a prison' theme – clearly it would have been worse under Fortinbras – a parade of military domination, armed guards, and so forth, ever a sense that through Elsinore doors were being locked, keys rattling. But this did impede Shakespeare. So did the evolutions of the cast who (memories of the Edinburgh Assembly Hall) rushed through the audience at any excuse. Burbage could have realised that, save for a greyness of tone which possibly afflicted him only at the première, Keith Michell – forty-four then – was technically exact and might conceivably have been a Prince. Yet he had no special hypnotic power, though I think of him now before such players as a Polonius who reminded me of a paranoiac major on parade snapping out the Precepts, and a Gravedigger (the parts were doubled) who was sepulchrally Dickensian, perhaps a salute to the Dickens tradition in Southwark. It made a change, I suppose. Though there was a Ghost who managed for ten minutes to be haunting on a fully-lighted stage, it was not an experiment to endear Bankside to a respectful visitor; it reiterated that the more one fiddles about with *Hamlet*, the more it loses. There is a passage in Chekhov's *Three Sisters* when the old porter talks for no reason at all of a contractor who told him that a rope was stretched right across the city of Moscow, 'What for?' somebody asks; and the porter replies, 'Don't know, sir, the contractor said so.' We feel at times that a rope is stretched across Elsinore, though nobody except the director knows why. Directors' caprices are by no means limited to *Hamlet*: I recall, from various years, two superfluous pipe organs installed in the Belmont of *The Merchant of Venice*; what appeared to be a motor rally at Verona in a modern-dress *Romeo and Juliet*; and a Macbeth speaking the entire Cauldron scene while tossing in a nightmare.

I found a foreign caprice during the spring of 1973. Romanian directors had been inquiring about recent revivals of *Hamlet*; but when, with Wendy, I went for the

British Council to Bucharest, nobody had planned a production among the impressive group of subsidised theatres; we were equally unfortunate on a return journey. On the first visit the show-piece was a debatably brilliant *Measure for Measure*, or *Mâsurâ Pentru Mâsurâ* – the decade's fashionable play – in a railway and industrial area, as it were a Willesden, on the fringe of the city. The director saw the narrative as a statement of corrupting power, all leading to the Duke's choice of Isabella, no perfunctory rounding-off but the last event in a relentless progress – another view of the power-game that, simplified, we had been seeing in the Bankside *Hamlet*. It had the effect of making me wish for a production in which nothing whatever was twisted to topicality.

IV

That wish was granted at Greenwich during the following spring, 1974. Here, in a retreat from the Shakespeare that, in accord with fashion, is interpreted in programme notes as well as on the stage, *Hamlet* was played practically straight: another face of Jonathan Miller. It made minor eccentricities more apparent: speech so colloquial that it was almost startling when the First Player declaimed or when Hamlet ranted at the graveside. Line after line was relaxed. Peter Eyre, urging himself on with words he did not credit, and stretched upon a bench to speak 'O, what a rogue and peasant slave' and other soliloquies, sounded as if Hamlet were barely breathing his thoughts. Miller had been bent on informality; we heard the night's opening words (the scene this time was uncut) spoken off-stage, missing the intense atmospheric quality. Hamlet was also unseen for a time while opening his advice to the Players. Relaxed or not, the text had been closely examined; there were unlooked-for emphases, such as the running-on, in

Hamlet's first soliloquy, of 'possess it merely that it should come to this'. Polonius, during the Precepts, chose the Second Quarto reading, 'courage' for 'comrade' ('Do not dull thy palm with entertainment / Of each new-hatch'd, unfledg'd courage'). The night could be seen as a confident, serviceable pocket edition. Peter Eyre, Robert Stephens' slippery Claudius, ultimately defiant, and Nicola Pagett's erotically agonised Ophelia, wearing black from the beginning, were in the vein; it seemed in keeping with Miller's season of 'family romances' (the other two were *Ghosts* and *The Seagull*) that the Closet scene, Irene Worth as Gertrude, lived more strongly than the rest.

Soon we would be advancing to a key period in any story of the twentieth-century stage, the National's opening in the three theatres, the Olivier, Lyttelton and the Cottesloe studio, at the great building on the South Bank. Elisabeth Scott's Shakespeare Memorial had been reviled at Stratford half a century before and then grew into an ancient monument. Similarly there appeared to be a plot – it died with the years – to blame Denys Lasdun for the grandeur of his National. Obviously there had to be an early *Hamlet* – on the Lyttelton's proscenium stage – and we saw it, in Peter Hall's revival, at the Old Vic before the final emigration. Hamlet was Albert Finney, in 1975 a man of thirty-seven, whom I remembered from his Birmingham years with Barry Jackson. Almost from drama school he played Henry V, a warrior for the working day, in the morning of his youth; and, at twenty-two, a Macbeth who kept emotional impetus until the last wave was dashed against the impermeable rock. Now, after sixteen years during which he had been as acclaimed as any British actor, he was playing Hamlet at full length for Peter Hall, Olivier's successor as head of the National. Hall had written in his diary (it was published years later): 'Don't we normally cut either to fit some preconceived theory for the production, or because we simply can't make the passage work? I think my future direction in Shakespeare must be to reveal the total object as well as possible.' (He did so superbly in his uncut *Antony and Cleopatra* at the Olivier in 1987.)

At *Hamlet* it could have been the right sign when, after two and a half hours of the entire text, he heard frantic debate during the interval. A last ovation was tumultuous; but the richest of theatrical experiences needs a Hamlet with a personality fit for the high heaven of the drama; it was hardly so when Finney, solid, bearded, questing, vastly intelligent and vibrantly spoken, gave us a Prince who did nothing paltry or mean, but who seldom pulled down the lightning. Remarkable here and there – he was a Hamlet who persuaded us that he saw the Ghost – usually sympathetic and assured in argument, I fancy that at Elsinore, whatever his uncle's view, he would have been a most popular Prince. Yet towards the close when, guiltily, I began to feel a lowering of the spirit, I had to quote to myself James Agate at another tragedy long ago: 'This piece of irony was capitally delivered; that litre of passion was neatly decanted; but we waited in vain for the onslaught on sensibility which should overthrow us quite.'

15

THAMES AND AVON:
1975–87

I

THE more we meet *Hamlet*, the more its revivals
fight together in the mind, scene by scene, speech
by speech, until in memory too little moves from
the chaos. Passionately, actors are re-inventing Hamlet
himself; directors, as passionately, re-invent the play for a
new generation which becomes too soon an old one and
makes room for yet another flurry. I have long doubted
whether the smallest phrase has been left entirely un-
considered. Though during the late 1970s and early 1980s
we saw traces of a reversion to a nearly primitive notion
that the play should take off in the theatre straight from the
text (but which text, and why?), some directors obsessed
by change sought still to commit the oldest sins in the
newest kind of ways.

There has been waywardness throughout the acted Folio;
but *Hamlet* has probably suffered most – not only in our
time – from the curiosities that have been part of its
entourage. Chance Newton, the veteran critic who called
himself 'Carados', recollected how a Victorian tragedian,
William Creswick, 'after each soliloquy would walk about
the stage three times and then "strike a picture" in the
middle'; how a troupe of pantomimists, disguised as
gravediggers, used to introduce a spade dance around

Ophelia's grave; and how a light-comedian Hamlet let
loose a dog at the King to pin him to earth. I am rather
surprised that this has not been copied. But Shakespeare's
collaborators have been otherwise engaged. During the
mid-1960s the tragedy was a mirror for disaffected youth
who may or may not have known that Hamlet's Wittenberg was a university of radical revolt. Later, Elsinore
would be a political devil's kitchen, the world's prison. All
stayed bitterly anti-heroic in the spirit of the decade, though
romanticism crept in again when new directors read the
score.

II

Early in 1976 a *Hamlet* done months before at the Other
Place, Stratford's Protean hut across the way from the
Royal Shakespeare Theatre, reached the dreariest of near-
basement studios, holding fewer than 200 people, in the
London Round House. My sole experience of this apart-
ment hardly encouraged me to return. The first and loved
director of the revival, Buzz Goodbody, had died four days
after its Stratford première. Now in the depths of Chalk
Farm the play was acted at a great pace on a very small,
shallow stage by about a dozen players in modern dress
against a simple neutral background. Ben Kingsley, then
thirty-two, sensitive to any nuance and quite unromantic,
never merely hovered over the surface of the text: this was
an intellectual at work, an animated mind, but I learned, as I
had feared, that the night would dissolve in memory. It was
right to speak trippingly on the tongue; less so, as with
many of the cast, to reduce the lines to colloquial patter:
instead of listening one strove to hear, a form of eavesdropping surprisingly familiar in a studio's intimacy. It was
a relief when Kingsley permitted himself full volume in
'How all occasions!', and I wished I had known him in an

Elsinore more propitious. Often the cast would roam in the aisles; there had seldom been a better Ghost than Griffith Jones, who could be an unearthly figure even when brushing past my left shoulder.

From the last dozen years I have omitted various remoter productions on which Osric might have pronounced 'Nothing, neither way'. (That ambiguous personage, once performed as the stupidest man at Court, was at least a fairly alert judge of fencing.) There had been hope during the 1970s for the future of a new Shakespeare theatre, St George's, in an unused church at the end of Tufnell Park Road in north London: not the easiest place to get at on a wet winter evening. Inside it had a neo-Elizabethan quality which satisfied the demanding Shakespearian, Robert Speaight; but after a few productions during which companies became easier to hear, pleasure thinned. Too few in a *Hamlet* cast (1977) valued the verse: mechanical routine supervened, and an often redoubtable actor, Alan Dobie, snapping through the part, had to remind me of a wire-haired terrier; like the Victorian dog, he might have turned at once upon Claudius with well-trained satisfaction. St George's continued to strive bravely through the seasons with no rewarding fortune.

III

The period's most regarded Hamlet (1977), on tour and at the Old Vic, was Derek Jacobi: the company, Toby Robertson's Prospect Theatre, had merited its quick popularity. Fourteen years earlier, Jacobi had been in three productions with which the Birmingham Repertory completed its full Shakespeare record; to be cast as Aaron in *Titus Andronicus*, Troilus and Henry VIII was variety enough and we did not wonder that he went straight to Olivier's National company at the Vic as Laertes to

O'Toole's Hamlet; he was there through Olivier's reign, modest, adaptable, and waiting. When the Prospect *Hamlet* arrived there were the customary and foolish suppositions that Jacobi must have sprung, fully armed, from a television serial; in fact, few men had had a more potent theatre experience. At thirty-eight he was neither an aspiring undergraduate nor a peevish youth fitted better to a street corner than the Danish throne. Logical, graceful, possibly the most touching Hamlet since John Neville, but fortified always by his fiery spirit, he re-charged my faith in the courtier's, soldier's, scholar's eye, tongue, sword. To listen to him was like reading the play in a fresh format: no emphases were follow-my-leader. Some matters in the three-hour version I questioned: such an improbability as speaking 'To be, or not to be' directly to Ophelia; during the Play scene the wearing of a snatched-up mask. I regretted the loss of 'How all occasions', lines that had hung in the air of the Old Vic since Olivier in 1937 and were lost now because the Prospect *Hamlet* had been based upon the Folio text, with omissions suggested by the First Quarto.

Toby Robertson's organisation was thorough, even if I wished that he had taken us into the play immediately, at 'Who's there?' on the frost-bound guard platform instead of at a prefatory parade, before the curtain, of King and Queen, Hamlet and Ghost. During the Council scene a splenetic Claudius (Timothy West) showed, not unnaturally, his angry impatience with Hamlet dozing in the corner. Hamlet read 'What a piece of work is a man!' from a book; the King's 'Madness in great ones must not unwatch'd go' was a quick explanatory farewell to Ophelia; yet again the Claudius-Laertes plot was transferred to the end of the Graveyard scene. We had no cause to ask how 'Look here upon this picture and on this' would be pointed, for portraits of the dead King and Claudius were permanently upon the walls: Gertrude (a grand Shakespearian,

Barbara Jefford) stood in her folly and sudden self-knowledge above the remainder of a cast that mostly re-burnished the play.

Revised, the production reappeared at the Vic before its company went on a world tour, opening in Denmark. Jacobi's searching performance had been altered, not altogether for the better, to explore Hamlet's antic disposition 'in the context of the King's description of the exterior madness as a turbulent and dangerous lunacy'. Robert Eddison's Polonius, stroking every inflection, prompted a veteran playgoer to say that she had never felt sorrier than when the old man fell dead behind the arras.

IV

Not far from the Old Vic, on the other side of The Cut, is the severe, workaday auditorium of the Young Vic where events can vary, at a director's whim, between the stirring, the rare (Byron's *Marino Faliero*), and now and then the odd. An acting area, hemmed by the audience on three sides, has the obvious advantages and disadvantages inseparable from extreme intimacy. Michael Bogdanov, in charge during the autumn of 1977, knew how to use the space, but he may have puzzled young listeners with *Hamlet* as part of a three-play sequence that also covered *Richard III* and *The Tempest* under the collective label of 'Action Man'. A programme note, affirming that 'the struggle for power, be it the Crown of England, the Throne of Denmark, or the Dukedom of Milan, is the theme of this trilogy', observed helpfully that Hamlet was 'unable either to opt in or cop out', a phrase made for a crossword. The editor found space, too, for King Edward VIII's abdication broadcast, cuttings from the onset of the Second World War, photographs of some unphotogenic people 'convicted in bugging case', and comments on *Hamlet* from a mixed bran-tub: one by Professor Kott ('Politics hangs here over every feeling; all the characters are poisoned by it') and one, from an English source, hardly designed to grace an exam paper: 'Hamlet is a slob . . . How can anyone talk so pretty in a rotten country with the sort of work he's got cut out for him?'

Nothing of this was a gilt-edged invitation to a masterpiece. The performance was not really enlightening, though (as I remember) I would not have dismissed Philip Bowen, moderate and intelligent in gold-rimmed spectacles, as a slob. Opting in or copping out, he had to be at the core of a power-game revival seldom marked by a sensitive respect for its dramatist. Ophelia (no room for favour or prettiness) went mad aggressively; the Gravediggers were let loose, and the duel scene – Mr Bogdanov's volatility unrestrained – was embroidered by a whistling moron and a comic band. I believe that the King wore a paper hat.

Of two other Young Vic *Hamlets*, by different directors, one (1982) lingers for the concentration and temperate wisdom of Edward Fox. A second (1985) also left one unclouded memory, Heather Canning's Queen: in the Closet scene she expressed without exaggeration (some actresses think they must make a meal of the passage) the woman's fear, affection and weakness. The production was in modern dress, a manner frequently excused, or glorified, as more accessible (to whom?). A fluent Hamlet, Matthew Marsh, having digested his own advice not to o'erstep the modesty of nature, was prepared to sacrifice imaginative relish to rapid naturalism. Ophelia (Natasha Richardson) had not the heart-stopping quality, but that would come. There was a power-game programme note by a university lecturer: 'The rottenness of the state of Denmark which nauseates Hamlet is the stinking corruption of politics in the early seventeenth century . . . Elsinore is the world's first modern totalitarian state.' More useful was that rare programme inclusion, a synopsis of playing time: 'Act One (approximately 45 minutes), 7 or 8 weeks after the death of King Hamlet, duration of action about 28 hours; Act Two (approximately 1 hour 40 minutes), about two months later, duration of action about two days; Act Three (approximately one hour), 3 or 4 days later, duration of action about 24 hours.'

Out in Sloane Square the Royal Court Theatre has been since 1956 the centre of stage rebellion, not what it was but always at the centre of a tempting cause. Shakespeare has not been among its major causes. A *Hamlet* (1980) might have been summarised as 'The Case of the Intrusive Director', by no means a continuing label for Richard Eyre (who in 1988 is to follow Peter Hall at the National Theatre). The loss of the great opening had become commonplace: no frigid darkness, formal challenge, tingling nerves, or apparition that 'bodes some strange eruption to our state'. I feared the worst when, on entering, I saw the stage occupied by a semi-ecclesiastical set vaguely resembling choir stalls. Then into the fight: the 'sweet prince' on his path to the future would be an unmanned neurotic. Trouble began when, instead of seeing the Ghost, he was possessed by it and spoke its lines. Jonathan Pryce had the merits of aspect, intensity, domination, but he had to bear with much. Thus, at the arrival of the Players, he was condemned to listen to an unnecessary and poorly written and delivered re-casting of the Hecuba speech. Almost as peculiar was the staging of the Graveyard scene in a charnel-house, or ossuary, so shelved with skulls that any gravedigger required a trained memory. In his most express-ive scenes (when he was not swallowing the end of a line) we could appreciate Pryce's understanding of what he had to do. One approving critic, and there were many of these, saw him as 'a bundle of sweaty, ferocious humanity', no doubt the 'sweating ferocity of the fair state'. Pryce was better than that.

V

According to the latest Stratford performances, the new
decade at the Danish Court might be quieter ('Let be').
Michael Pennington (1980) was never a trendy symbol but
a man (aged thirty-seven) with a probing intelligence, the
'noble heart' of Horatio's epitaph, and speech that rejected
merely novel point-making. He could be passion's slave as
well. A problem was what we might remember from him:
he lacked an actor's preservative, mesmeric authority. Even
so, if there was little enough for permanency, on the night it
was playing clean and civilised: epithets for John Barton's
production which moved from a matter-of-course opening
– would Barnardo have appeared like a jack-in-the-box
from the cellarage? – to full realisation of the tragedy.
Pennington, unlike some actors, knew the value of
narrative suspense (a pity that so few can be surprised by
Hamlet). In a *Drama* article (Summer 1981) he wrote:

> I like the story inordinately, and agree with my mother
> when she hopes against hope every time that Hamlet will
> turn down that challenge of Osric's and live; and I also
> think for instance that if we didn't know the damned
> thing so well, the inspiration in Shakespeare to write a
> comedy scene by an open grave that turns out to be that
> of the protagonist's lover, immediately between the
> setting of a deadly plot and its upspringing, would be
> seen for the breath-taking audacity that it is.

Now, after scores of nights, I wait first for legitimate
excitement, scenes to add to the pattern of an ideal
performance created through the years. In constant repet-
ition there has been too little to cherish. Often Ron
Daniels's Stratford revival (1984), in its greys and blacks,
could only grumble along, though Roger Rees, at his
emotional pitch, presented a distraught Prince, prompted

by heaven and hell to discoveries in the world and in his own grief that he had not contemplated. If as a rule the revelation was direct, there could be tracts when Rees was too enmeshed in his discoveries to describe them to us lucidly. Yet not (in the audience) an occasion for melancholy unbridled. One small matter. I was glad to find that here the Polonius, Laertes and Ophelia might have come from the same family instead of being brought together fortuitously at author and director's bidding.

VI

I cannot think that Ingmar Bergman, who directed *Hamlet* for the Royal Swedish Theatre, a production which came during June 1987 to the Lyttelton Theatre of the National, bothered much about the play's problems, major or minor. 'When the mystery of Hamlet has been solved, the mystery of human life will have been solved,' the critic Harold Child wrote in 1935. Bergman simply used familiar material for an intensely theatrical melodrama that lapsed into cynical violence when Fortinbras, as a ruthless thug, took possession of Elsinore. Horatio (of all people) was shot, off-stage, and the bodies of the King and Queen were thrust ignominiously through a trap – after which Fortinbras delivered his own closing speech for the benefit of television cameras.

The play in Bergman's treatment proved to be not so much the tragedy of Hamlet as the tragedy of Ophelia. Onwards, from her employment as bait in the Nunnery scene where she had the roughest experience, she haunted the stage at all times; in her madness offering bent nails instead of flowers, and being present even at her own funeral in the rain (where Bergman's choice of weather had been anticipated long before by Tyrone Guthrie). Throughout, an affecting actress, Pernilla Östergren, fortified emotion by technique. Hamlet (Peter Stormare), a resolutely physical performance, was obliged to go thoroughly over the top in the wildest of antic dispositions: this seemed to be developing from the moment when he arrived late at Court, hardly the 'mould of form' – noticeably, poor Ophelia's later description was cut – in dark glasses and a crumpled mackintosh, angrily tugging a bentwood chair, one of the few palace furnishings. On the battlements he readily entered the embrace of the yearning, if not particularly phantasmal, ghost of his father, who appeared in what resembled a dressing-gown, certainly not 'the very armour he had on when he the ambitious Norway combated'. Hamlet then proceeded to a tempestuous life, clutching at most people in sight and stabbing Polonius brutally through the eye. He could have been described, in a single simplification, as a lug-the-guts Hamlet, though at the end we had to respect him as an expert fencer.

This was, in any view, a brutal and corrupt Elsinore where the change of kingship appeared, in English terms, to be a move from Edward the Confessor to Henry VIII. The Ghost dropped in conveniently at the last to prop up his brother for Hamlet's disposal. A viciously sexual Claudius we saw first tumbling his infatuated Gertrude in front of a pack of courtiers (dressed in judicial robes and wigs) sycophantically applauding. It was also an eccentric Elsinore – the costumes were a medley – with Horatio looking like an Edwardian fop in a curly-brimmed bowler.

Though it all made a passionate melodrama, the production was another example of a director seizing upon the play for his own ends. Shakespeare might have murmured, 'Report me and my cause aright . . .'.

16
LIVING WITH HAMLET: 1916–87

I

DURING 1905 P. G. Wodehouse, then twenty-three, wrote the verses below which appeared in *Books of Today*. It was at a time when in London, within two months, H. B. Irving played Hamlet at the Adelphi as a naturally lovable figure embittered, and Martin Harvey was at the Lyric in an eleventh-century production, carefully archaeological. Provincial revivals, Frank Benson's for one, were frequent. Hence Wodehouse's 'Too Much Hamlet':

I went to book a ticket for to see a modern play;
The man behind the counter said, 'There's no such thing today,
Every actor who has any self-respect is being starred
In the brightly-written masterpiece of England's Only Bard.
　　　　It's 'Hamlet' here and 'Hamlet' there,
　　　　And 'Hamlet' on next week.
　　　An actor not in 'Hamlet' is regarded as a freak.

A pleasant farce with music would, I thought, be to my mind,
But not a single pleasant farce with music could I find.

At every theatre which I sought men answered with a
  bow,
'We've given up our farces. We are playing "Hamlet"
  now.'
       It's 'Hamlet' this, and 'Hamlet' that,
         And ' "Hamlet" – Mr Jones.'
   Our starving British dramatists are mainly skin and
    bones.

I went into a music-hall, but soon came out of it
On seeing some comedians in a painful 'Hamlet' skit,
And a gentleman who gave some imitations, all alone,
Of other people's Hamlets, plus a Hamlet of his own.
       It's 'Hamlet' this, and 'Hamlet' that,
         And 'Hamlet' day by day.
   Shakespeare and Bacon must regret they ever wrote
    the play.

I don't deny that 'Hamlet' has its merits as a play:
In many ways it's finer than the drama of today.
But with all respect to Bacon (and his colleague) I protest
That I think the British Public is entitled to a rest.
       It's 'Hamlet' here, and 'Hamlet' there,
         And ' "Hamlet" – Record Run.'
   It seems to me the masterpiece is being overdone.

Between that summer, when Wodehouse was writing so
cheerfully, and the early 1920s, there were several more
Hamlets. And since then? Let me summarise. To have lived
with the Hamlets of more than six decades is to have known
wholesale changes in performance, direction, management, theatres, settings, audiences. Actor-managers have
almost vanished. We have gone from the hand-to-mouth
financing of a provincial tour to official subsidies for such
companies as the National and the Royal Shakespeare and

the arrival of industrial sponsorship. In performance directors, all-powerful now and increasingly sophisticated, impose their wishes. Hamlet himself has largely shifted from the heart of a romantic-tragic narrative to a figure that speaks for its actor's own day, the time out of joint, the police state. Theatre architects have rejected the curtained proscenium for something like neo-Elizabethan austerity. Scene designers have long moved from the merely representational. Costumes are shifted over the centuries according to a director's whim. Audiences, informal and in general younger, accept the politics of Elsinore as those of their morning's newspaper.

There must always be a new Hamlet, though it is only since the Second World War that many of us have learned to live with the entire play, the 'eternity'. Once, with eight or ten curtain-down scenic changes – since forgotten in an age of the permanent set – Hamlet, as written, would have been too ambitious for normal production; actor-managers, who had to have the last word, were delighted to remove subsidiary characters (Fortinbras was doomed). The length of Hamlet's own part would vary with adjustments made to the First Folio text commonly used, but it has seldom been less than three times that of the King's. Guy Boas, the headmaster who directed much Shakespeare with his enthusiastic boys at Sloane School, Chelsea, showed me his length analysis of the *Hamlet* parts: it fascinated Michael Redgrave and today it inevitably crops up when I see a fresh production:

Hamlet, 1530 lines; Claudius, 524; Polonius, 338; Horatio, 265; Laertes, 185; Ophelia, 170; Queen, 133; First Gravedigger (or Clown), 105; Rosencrantz, 99; Ghost, 92; Osric, 54; Guildenstern, 53; First Player, 53; Player King, 48; Marcellus, 47; Barnardo, 32; Player Queen, 28; Fortinbras, 25; Voltimand, 21; Second

Gravedigger, 19; Priest, 12; A Lord, 12; Gentleman, 11; Captain, 11; Another Gentleman, 10; Reynaldo, 9; Francisco, 7; Ambassador, 7; Sailor, 5; Messenger, 4; Cornelius, 1; Servant, 1.

It took me a few years to live with the 'eternity' text. Even in this a stray phrase was likely to escape in performance: I know – but flagging attention may have defeated me – it seemed a long time before I heard Claudius say to Laertes, not that it mattered, when urging him flatteringly to the duel: 'The scrimers of their nation / He swore had neither motion, guard nor eye / If you oppos'd them.' A 'scrimer' is a fencer. (Even today I cannot be certain that I heard this.)

II

Cut or uncut, Prince Hamlet is the most eloquent of problems – 'talking, talking' a small-part actor, who was probably a thwarted Cornelius, said to me enviously long ago. Seldom alike in consecutive revivals, he can be affected by the mood of the day. It was not so during the mid-1890s when Gordon Craig, Ellen Terry's son, wondered if the part could be acted with a black patch over one eye: 'People are sick and tired of seeing the same Hamlet sitting in the same chair, with no marked sign of difference from any Hamlet seen before.' Craig, incorrigibly restless, was speaking with the voice of directors far into the future. In a broad simplification, from an introspective, deeply melancholy romantic, Hamlet would become either a Freudian son, a bleak agnostic student, a desperate neurotic, or a wholly restless avenger. Especially in the second half of this century directors have sought to remove him from the large effects that troop with majesty to the picture of a young man glumly pottering about in the vague hope of doing something but not immediately. Living out his days in a world of death and burial, he can be anyone his latest actor, from a similarly grievous world outside the theatre, chooses to think. Rather than 'His life was gentle' the likeliest clue during the 1960s and 1970s would have been 'I'll lug the guts into the neighbour room'.

I valued Boas's record because the most minor people in the play have always fascinated me. The Prince rules; but I have never wished characters he hardly noticed to be dismissed with a casual 'etc.': they belong to the fabric. Cornelius, one of the ambassadors to Norway (with Voltimand) is the smallest: it was years before I met him and began to brood idly on the poor fellow who has only ten words which he shares (I.2) with his senior: 'In that, and all things, will we show our duty.' Maybe a diffident functionary who would have got no higher in the Diplomatic Service because of a maddening failure to express himself in public.

Cornelius has often doubled or trebled with other footnote-parts; at the Westminster in 1937 he was also Francisco and a wordless Second Sailor. Francisco, plain soldier, is present at the very beginning of the midnight watch: we know nothing personal except that he is susceptible to cold and on the winter night is 'sick at heart'. Dover Wilson has said, implausibly I think, that 'the solitary figure, with his heart-sickness, foreshadows Hamlet.' Did that really occur to Shakespeare? Another tiny part, Reynaldo (II.1) foreshadows nobody in particular and could be any convenient Gentleman: Alec Guinness rediscovered him in 1937, a self-contained young man adroitly tactful as he defers to Polonius. In an 'eternity' cast he could have doubled under the pseudonym of 'Walter Plinge', a name borrowed by the Bensonian, H. O. Nicholson, from the name of an innkeeper near the Lyceum.

The churlish Priest at Ophelia's funeral can also be doubled. There is argument about this cleric. An expert has said that he should wear 'a gown and tippet over his cassock and a square cap as ordered by the canon of 1604', the tippet being what we call a black scarf. A rigid personage, no doubt a terror in his parish, he would have continued in his fuss about the garlands and flowers granted to Ophelia, 'her virgin crants, her maiden strewments', customary at a girl's burial but here profaning the service of the dead.

III

Modern ideas of the Elsinore these people knew so well might baffle them. In the theatre the castle has been built and rebuilt, most lavishly in the huge Gothic structures of Charles Kean, Fechter, Irving, and Tree. They were Victorian. In my time the setting has varied between the conventionally romantic – fit for a mullioned window against which Wolfit died at Stratford – an open space furnished by a single arras, and in 1970 (as Sally Beauman has described in her history of the Royal Shakespeare Company) 'an oppressive chamber set, roofed and walled with Venetian blinds which could, theoretically, convert the entire staging from white to black in the twinkling of an eye, but which proved either to stick or, merely, revolve to the accompaniment of loud mechanical whirrings'. When scenery was too, too solid, its change would be a protracted evolution. Now furniture is employed less and less except perhaps for a pair of thrones and not invariably for them. 'Have we no cheers?' asks the Vice Chancellor in Pinero's *Trelawny of the 'Wells'*; and again and again we have wished for a chair or so to hint at a certain amount of gracious living.

There remains the question of the Queen's bed. 'My lord,' says Polonius to the King, 'he is going to his mother's closet – behind the arras I'll convey myself.' A bed in the Closet is superfluous; it is never mentioned, though fashion has been tilting that way. Professor Arthur Colby Sprague has said (*Shakespeare's Plays Today*) that it would have been, in the Elizabethan meaning of the word, simply a private room. He adds that a chair is conspicuous in such a famous early picture as one that accompanies the tragedy in Rowe's edition of 1709. During the 1920s an austere couch or sofa was added to the chair. 'Meanwhile critical interest in the sexual and even Freudian aspects of the play has been mounting. It is in keeping that what used to be known as the Closet Scene became "the Bedroom Scene" in Dover Wilson's *What Happens in Hamlet* (1935). An actual bed, predictably, was introduced in Gielgud's brilliant *Hamlet* in New York the next year. (Earlier, in London, the actor had suggested one, by means of curtains.) By 1950 Kenneth Tynan was wondering *why* "there should be a bed stage centre in every production of this scene. It is never mentioned and never slept in".'

The quality of speech is more important than a piece of furniture. I have always welcomed an actor who looks for the music, though there is a reaction today against something despised, unselectively, as 'the voice beautiful'. A character in Jonathan Griffin's fine play, *The Hidden King* (about Sebastian of Portugal) says: 'You see, I do not hate the splendour': it is a charged phrase I commend to any director who seeks modishly to blur *Hamlet* as an exercise in abrasiveness. I have seldom quoted in this book, so here is a portion of the advice to the Players, as topical as it ever was:

Speak the speech, I pray you, as I pronounc'd it to you, trippingly on the tongue; but if you mouth it, as many of our players do, I had as lief the town-crier spoke my lines. Nor do not saw the air too much with your hand, thus, but use all gently; for in the very torrent, tempest, and, as I may say, whirlwind of your passion, you must acquire and beget a temperance that may give it smoothness. O, it offends me to the soul to hear a robustious, periwig-coated fellow tear a passion to tatters, to very rags, to split the ears of the groundlings, who, for the most part, are capable of nothing but inexplicable dumb shows and noise . . .

Be not too tame neither, but let your own discretion be your tutor. Suit the action to the word, the word to the action; with this special observance, that you o'erstep not the modesty of nature . . .

Though unashamedly fond of lists, it would be perilous for me to place in any firm order the major Hamlets I have known. But certain passages for a composite performance which would be my nonpareil stay with me in the voices of their speakers. One is Gielgud's 'There are more things in heaven and earth, Horatio, than are dreamt of in your *philosophy*', avoiding the snubbing intonation – impossible with this actor – where a minor Hamlet would come down like a load of bricks on 'your'. Then Ernest Milton's astonished 'amaze indeed the very faculties of eyes and ears'; Scofield's urgency (in his first Stratford performance) at 'Mother, for love of grace, lay not that flattering unction to your soul'; Olivier's desperation at 'I do not know / Why yet I live to say / This thing's to do' (in that soliloquy perfection has as many faces as Hamlet himself); and the abstracted quietness of George Hayes in his last talk with Horatio when Osric has left them. I recollect an innominate Gentleman who brought (in an Old Vic revival) news of Ophelia's madness to the Queen. Actions come back: Richard Pasco hurtling the throne-chair from the dais at the climax of 'O, what a rogue and peasant slave'; Donald Wolfit (Stratford, 1936), after the Ghost's 'Remember me!', lying on his back – business that derived, I think, from

Forbes-Robertson in 1896 – and gazing at the night sky, 'O all you host of heaven!'; and in Budapest Miklós Gábor, before an audience as rapt as any I have known, raising himself for a moment on his elbow at 'The rest is silence' and falling back to death.

IV

To have lived with *Hamlet* in the theatre is to have lived not with the people of the play alone and those who have acted in it and watched it, but also some whose voices are now silent. I never saw Ion Swinley as Hamlet (his fame was at the Vic) but in so much else that I can nearly map his performance: among superb speakers of the English theatre he was a man of grace and settled melancholy. With the players are men who were writing of them during my first thirty years in London: Ivor Brown, giving his quick double nod as he sat (for too brief a time) in his editorial chair; W. A. (Bill) Darlington, gently searching his memory and regretting he had missed John Philip Kemble; Lionel Hale, a mercurial presence; Eric Keown, glancing wryly at the John Knox statue as we walked up to the Edinburgh Assembly Hall; Victor Cookman concentrating on the stage without making a note; Philip Hope-Wallace strolling from the theatre to find a telephone and extemporise his review. Players, colleagues, friends, they return, fade, return: a movement, a cadence, a comment. With them, too, the theatres: newer spaces (that they did not know) of the South Bank and Barbican; the friendly embrace of the Old Vic; the West End's intermittent welcome; a theatre that through half a century has grown into its Avonside meadow; nutshell-studios, halls on the outer fringe; the Marienlyst ballroom on a night of pelting rain; the Picture House of the Stratford interregnum.

Further back, when London was far off, the Plymouth

theatre, now simply a name, light beyond its Ionic columns; street lamps across a vanished city; the first Hamlets, Darch, Baynton, Milton; the first exchanges ('Who's there?' – 'Nay, answer me') in the shivering night of Elsinore. Far beyond that again, December darkness, a crash of waves on the full face of Old Lizard Head, the striking of a grandfather clock, a book that fell from an upper shelf; nights of perplexity, discovery, astonishment, in a waking world; and always the challenge and answer, 'Stand, ho! Who is there?' – 'Friends to this ground . . . and liegemen to the Dane'.

BIBLIOGRAPHY

Addenbrooke, David, *The Royal Shakespeare Company* (William Kimber, 1974)

Agate, James, *Brief Chronicles* (Cape, 1943)

Alexander, Peter (ed), *William Shakespeare: The Complete Works* (Collins, 1951)

Beauman, Sally, *The Royal Shakespeare Company* (Oxford, 1982)

Boas, Guy, *Shakespeare and the Boy Actors* (Barrie and Rockliff, 1962 ed)

Brown, Ivor, *Shakespeare* (Collins, 1949)

Campbell, Oscar James, and Quinn, Edward, *The Reader's Encyclopedia of Shakespeare* (Thomas Y. Crowell, New York, 1966)

Gielgud, Sir John, *Early Stages* (Macmillan, 1939)

Gilder, Rosamond, *John Gielgud's Hamlet* (Methuen, 1937)

Goodwin, John (ed), *Peter Hall's Diaries: The Story of a Dramatic Battle* (Hamish Hamilton, 1983)

Granville-Barker, Harley, *Prefaces to Shakespeare: Third Series, Hamlet* (Sidgwick and Jackson, 1937)

Harwood, Ronald (ed), *The Ages of Gielgud* (Hodder & Stoughton, 1984); *Sir Donald Wolfit, CBE* (Secker & Warburg, 1971)

Holmes, Martin, *The Guns of Elsinore* (Chatto & Windus, 1964)

Jenkins, Harold (ed), *Hamlet*: Arden Shakespeare edition (Methuen, 1982)

Lloyd Evans, Gareth and Barbara, *Everyman's Companion to Shakespeare* (Dent, 1978)

Mander, Raymond, and Mitchenson, Joe, *Hamlet Through the Ages* (Barrie and Rockliff, 1952)

O'Connor, Garry (ed), *Olivier: In Celebration* (Hodder & Stoughton, 1987)

Redgrave, Sir Michael, *The Actor's Ways and Means* (Heinemann, 1953)

Rowse, A. L., *William Shakespeare* (Macmillan, 1963)

Speaight, Robert, *Shakespeare on the Stage* (Collins, 1973)

Sprague, Arthur Colby, *Shakespeare and the Actors: The Stage Business In His Plays* (Harvard, Cambridge, Mass, 1944); (with J. C. Trewin)

Shakespeare's Plays Today: Some Customs and Conventions of the Stage (Sidgwick and Jackson, 1970)

Trewin, J. C., *Benson and the Bensonians* (Barrie and Rockliff, 1960); *Shakespeare on the English Stage 1900–1964* (Barrie and Rockliff, 1964); *Going to Shakespeare* (George Allen & Unwin, 1978)

Wells, Stanley (ed), *Shakespeare: Select Bibliographical Guides* (Oxford, 1973); and Gary Taylor (eds) *William Shakespeare: The Complete Works* (Oxford, 1986)

Wilson, J. Dover, (ed) *Hamlet*, New Cambridge Shakespeare (Cambridge, 1934); *What Happens in Hamlet* (Cambridge, 1935)

Index